Spinster Tales
and Womanly Possibilities

SPINSTER TALES

AND

WOMANLY POSSIBILITIES

NAOMI BRAUN ROSENTHAL

STATE UNIVERSITY OF NEW YORK PRESS

Published by
STATE UNIVERSITY OF NEW YORK PRESS,
ALBANY

© 2002 State University of New York

For information, address
State University of New York Press
90 State Street, Suite 700, Albany, NY 12207

Production and book design, Laurie Searl
Marketing, Anne M. Valentine

Library of Congress Cataloging-in-Publication Data

Rosenthal, Naomi Braun, 1940–
     Spinster tales and womanly possibilities / Naomi Braun Rosenthal.
         p.   cm.
     Includes bibliographical references and index.
     ISBN 0-7914-5205-0 (alk. paper). — ISBN 0-7914-5206-9 (pbk. : alk. paper)
     1. American fiction—History and criticism.   2. Women and literature—United States—History.   3. Feminist fiction, American—History and criticism.   4. Single women in literature.   5. Women in motion pictures.   6. Single women—Fiction. I. Title.

PS374.W6 R67 2002
813.009'920652—dc21   2001048346

10 9 8 7 6 5 4 3 2 1

to my family,
who prefer Jane Austen

CONTENTS

PREFACE

Although this book is a history, it contains little detailed information about real people or their lives. And while I try to describe a changing reality here, my subject—the twentieth-century spinster—was a figment of popular imagination. But the fact that the spinster was largely imagined hardly renders her insignificant. Far from it! Spinster imagery had a very real impact on living, breathing men and women. And that is the essence of my tale.

The spinster, who was once a common figure in American popular culture, has all but vanished from the scene. But her disappearance seems to have gone unnoticed and that is what makes it so intriguing. This book describes the reasons for her demise through an investigation of some of the stories that were told about her.

During the course of the twentieth century, she was successively depicted as: the model of a modern career woman; independent and socially useful if sometimes limited, lonely, or even selfish; successful in worldly terms but sexually frozen, incomplete, and excluded on that account; and latterly, unloved and unlovely. Invoked as a symbol of female independence at the turn of the century when marriage and career were considered to be incompatible choices for women, spinsterhood was advocated as an alternate path by some and viewed as a threat to family life by others. But as career options for married women expanded after World War I, claims that the spinster represented a superior form of womanhood dissipated, and the glamour of the celibate career woman was increasingly undermined by a new set of understandings of sexuality. Even so, it was not until World War II that the most negative images of spinsters began to proliferate. In the ensuing years, even as the number of women who eschewed marriage and avoided sexual activity decreased, the character that had once been portrayed as the epitome of independent, talented, and self-sufficient womanhood came to figure as the nightmare alternative for young women. And so she remained, despised and feared, until a new women's movement finished her off.

Today, there are few traces of the spinster's existence—the options open to women have changed dramatically. Still, we continue to grapple with concerns about the desires and needs of men and women and "the future of the family." Thinking about the spinster and her past may help to clarify some of possibilities for dealing with those issues.

I owe a debt of thanks to a number of people. Robert Zussman and Nancy Tomes have provided crucial input at every stage. They read my proposal, wrote letters of recommendation supporting the project, and then read the first painful draft of the manuscript. Nancy, Robert, and Ira Livingston gave me both helpful pointers for revision and the kind of encouragement that kept me working. I hope I have lived up to at least some of their expectations. Three anonymous readers for State University of New York Press also made very useful suggestions that guided me as I completed the manuscript. Ruth Elizabeth (Sue) Bottigheimer, Amanda Frisken, Joel Rosenthal, and Claire Meirowitz gave me detailed comments on the second draft. I am especially grateful for their pains and collegiality. Thanks also to Laura Anker, Ned Landsman, Patricia Roos, William R. Taylor, and Fred Weinstein, who mentored, sponsored, and aided me in this endeavor as in others. And I want to express my gratitude to Wangechi Mutu for the fine drawings that grace chapter 8.

I would not have had the time to complete the research for this project much less get far enough into the writing process to complete the book without the kindness of strangers. The gift of a Fellowship for College Teachers and Independent Scholars from the National Endowment for the Humanities provided a welcome salary supplement and convinced a reluctant administration to grant me a sabbatical during the 1995/96 academic year. In addition, the cost of the illustrations included in this volume were underwritten through small grants from Old Westbury's Presidential Grants Program and the PDQWL Program of the State University of New York Press Faculty/Staff union, the United University Professions.

I am very lucky to have had supportive colleagues in the American Studies Department at the State University of New York College at Old Westbury who have long encouraged me to think about a book-length project. I am also profoundly grateful for the courtesy appointment, office facilities, and collegial support provided me by the Sociology Department at the State University of New York at Stony Brook. Thanks too to the editors at SUNY Press who are taking a chance on this book and to the Press's helpful and gracious production staff.

Almost all scholars need help in locating and obtaining research materials and I, certainly no exception to that rule, would have been lost without the generous aid of the indefatigable librarians and staff at the State University of New York Press libraries at Old Westbury and Stony Brook, and the Port Jefferson Free Library Association.

Finally I want to publicly acknowledge my debts to Joel Rosenthal, who has been a source of financial and moral support for close to forty years and, more often than not, a diverting companion.

ONE

THE PERSISTENT SPINSTER

THIS BOOK DESCRIBES the circumstances that surrounded the puzzling life and death of an American icon. Who was she? Variously called "spinster," "old maid," or "bachelorette," and once, in the 1950s, named "reluctant virgin" by a counseling priest,[1] she was a woman who had become culturally important as a direct result of her marital status, or, more precisely, its lack.

That once-ubiquitous figure has all but vanished from our collective imagination. But like the dog whose failure to bark in the night proved so critical to Sherlock Holmes in the case of the *Silver Blaze*,[2] the fact that her disappearance has been both unnoticed and unaccounted for is, in itself, revealing. It represents an instance of what might be called a significant absence. Just as explaining the dog's unusual quiescence pointed to one perpetrator and away from other possibilities in Holmes' case, the investigation of what might, in another genre, be titled "the case of the persistent spinster" provides a key to a broader historical enigma, calling attention to a series of rapid transformations in attitudes toward women and the meaning of womanhood during the course of this century that culminated in an explosion of feminist insurgency during the late 1960s.

As is generally the case in the classic detective story, explaining how the spinster met her end involves recounting her history as well as the events leading up to her disappearance. Therefore, in the following pages I reveal the fruits of my investigation into the life and times of this interesting character. That story, like other fictional tales, details the elements of the protagonist's character and the circumstances involved in her demise, accounting for the details of both her victories and her defeats over the course of the last hundred years or so.

But there is more. The spinster is akin to the protagonists dreamed up by mystery writers in another way as well. She never actually walked the earth. Despite that circumstance, however, she wielded considerable influence over the lives of very real people. For that very reason, the reconstruction of the spinster's story—the consistencies and alterations in her appearance, the utterances of her friends and enemies, the threats she was reputed to present to established interests, and the forces that occasioned her unremarked, if somewhat belated, exit from the scene—is valuable as much for the insights it offers into twentieth-century debates about women in general as for its revelations about women who remained unmarried.

Spinster portraiture was accomplished by the efforts of several generations of rebels as well as traditionalists; inscribed and tested through the agency of the mass media; and codified and revised according to audience reactions. In consequence, the subject's lineaments were always in flux, altering alongside transformations in the surrounding cultural landscape. Despite the changes in iconography, however, the never-marrying woman occupied a prominent cultural niche, and her longevity as a subject of popular attention reflects a continuing preoccupation with the model. In the chapters that follow, I look at the reasons for the continuing appeal of spinster imagery and argue that the revision and eventual disappearance of this iconographic figure was connected to a larger set of transformations in twentieth-century myths and concerns.

My interest in the cultural history of women who remained single had its genesis in an earlier project—an analysis of the organizational connections of several groups of nineteenth-century women reformers. As I looked at the career patterns of a group of notable New York women activists of the period, I found that fewer than three-quarters of their number had ever married.[3] I also discovered, in looking at both comments of the time and histories of the period, that the accomplishments of the spinsters among that group had been at least partially contingent on freedom from marital entanglement. Yet, thinking about these celebrities of the early part of the century, I realized that, at least in childhood, my own attitude toward unmarried professional women had been far less than admiring. Born in 1940, just before the United States entered the war against the Axis powers, I came of age in a period noted for its celebration of domestic life. Perhaps in consequence, I remember pitying unmarried women for what I believed they lacked, rather than admiring them for what they might have achieved. I not only looked askance at women who stayed single; I feared the prospect of becoming one of their number. My apprehensions, as I remember them now, centered on what I was told and came to imagine as the deficiencies of that state and what I read into their lives and personalities. Some of the teachers in my elementary school and one of my aunts were spinsters. My schoolmates and I thought of those women in terms of their inadequacies, abnormalities, and peculiarities; we never even contemplated the possibility that they might be regarded as successful. Their accomplishments were invisible; their limitations obvious, at least to us. As to my aunt, her story, framed by her as a kind of Victorian tragedy and by my mother (in Freudian terms) as a neurotic flight from femininity, emphasized personal abnormality. Although she had attracted several suitors and even a proposal or two, she was described as either too sensitive to marry (her account) or unable to contemplate a "normal" relationship with a man (my mother's version). She had become a librarian, which all parties agreed was undoubtedly a consequence, rather than a cause, of these propensities.

I was hardly alone in holding these attitudes. Historian Linda Gordon, for example, has said that "nearly every woman" of the postwar generation felt the "terror of being a spinster."[4] Nancy Peterson, author of a book on single women, describes similarly negative attitudes among her circle of college friends in the early 1960s:

> We thought we knew what the alternative to marriage was. We thought we saw it in the familiar yet threatening facade of spinsterhood, exemplified in the glimpses we had of the lives of our unmarried college instructors, whom we often admired personally and certainly respected professionally, but whose dinner invitations to gracious but modest apartments, whose trips to professional conferences here and there, whose summer vacations spent in the Rockies with each other or with aged relatives only projected an image which chilled us.

Peterson's memory of her single women teachers in grade school was far less affectionate. After detailing some of their notable eccentricities, she concluded, "No, we knew what staying single meant, and we didn't want any part of it."[5]

I certainly viewed that estate as a consequence of and precursor to personal and psychological disaster. I thus avoided all choices that might lead to such a fate. In my mind that included: attending a woman's college, giving up opportunities to meet men by studying too assiduously, pursing a demanding career such as medicine, or entering a profession with a reputation for giving shelter to large numbers of unmarried women, such as librarianship. Keeping one's intellectual and professional reach from imperiling one's marital prospects was not, however, enough. Until I learned differently, I felt impelled to emulate, however amateurishly, the kind of femininity that I believed made marriage possible.

Those constructions from my childhood resonated very poorly with what I learned in the course of my research. Contemporaries certainly did not regard the women I had been studying as failures. Far from it, women such as organizer Susan B. Anthony, settlement house founder Lillian Wald, and poet Alice Cary had been celebrities in their own time. That led me to wonder about the causes and consequences of the changing imagery of spinsterhood. At the same time I also realized, with some surprise, just how rare present-day invocations of spinsterhood had become. While some actual spinsters may still exist, they no longer occupy significant cultural space in the United States. So, even though an occasional old maid turns up in those somewhat mannered, and one suspects self-consciously anachronistic, fictions, such as the repressed and timid secretary who figures tangentially in the plot of P. D. James's *Innocence House*, they are not consequential. And although there has been an attempt in the radical lesbian community to reclaim the spinster as a heroic figure, that can be accomplished only by ignoring one of the features that once defined her—her habitual sexual abstinence.[6]

Yet the spinster has little relevance or significance for young people nowadays. The figure that variously inspired, amused, and haunted audiences in the past has become both improbable and unbelievable in the eyes of the current generation. I came to appreciate this fact shortly after I began work on this book when I asked some of my students in an American Studies class to try to decode the rhetorical aims of a group of turn-of-the-century autobiographical statements. The group reporting on Anna Howard Shaw (the first woman minister ordained by the Methodist Protestant Church, a noted lecturer, and a prime mover in the struggle for women's suffrage)[7] said, without any hesitancy, that Shaw wanted to make clear she was a lesbian. When I asked them how they arrived at that conclusion, they said it was obvious because she never mentioned any heterosexual relationships and never married. I pointed out that that the reading included no material that even hinted at a homosexual orientation; Shaw made no mention of any romantic friendships with other women in the portion of the autobiography they were discussing. Instead, in these chapters, Shaw stressed her strong will, desire for independence, and early assumption of responsibility. Therefore, I suggested, rather than signaling an erotic preference for women, she might have wanted to explain why she never married and, I added, she might have been celibate. The students reacted dubiously to such a possibility even when I reminded them of the still-current requirement of Catholic nuns. They agreed it was possible that someone might *try* to abstain from erotic activity, but they had questions about the capacity of "normal" women to endure continuing sexual abstinence.

My sense that there has been a dramatic change in sexual sensibilities was reinforced by a discussion that I had with one of my cousins about my own ninety-year-old maiden aunt. In the course of that conversation, I said that, given my present interests, I would dearly love to ask my aunt about her sex life. But, I added, I could not bring myself to do so because the assumption that she had none was so much a part of our relationship that I could not even begin to interrogate her about erotic inclinations. Overhearing this conversation, my cousin's sixteen-year-old daughter reacted with vociferous disbelief to the very possibility that any woman might live a whole lifetime and yet be sexually inexperienced.

I recounted my young cousin's comments shortly afterward to a slightly younger colleague (for some reason now lost to me) and he, in turn, told me of his own shocked reaction to the discovery that an unmarried aunt—who, he said, "I just assumed was sexually inactive"—had actually had a long-term affair with a married man. This countertale suggested that while both of us had accepted a link between remaining single and sexual inactivity, members of a younger generation see no such likelihood. Young women of my past may have recoiled from what was assumed to be a specter of lifelong sexual abstinence; today they reject the very possibility of its existence.

After these encounters, I came to appreciate how culturally irrelevant the idea of spinsterhood has become. At the same time, I began to suspect that—given the dramatic changes women have effected in recent years—this instance of cultural amnesia, losing the memory of a formerly significant feature of social life, must reflect a deep shift in meaning.[8] And, as I pursued the question, I concluded that most traces of the once-powerful representations of single women have been so thoroughly effaced that no one seems to have even noted when or why they vanished. The never-marrying celibate has been so completely erased from popular representation that even the terminology that once identified her has either disappeared or lost its symbolic impact.

If her former importance, as I contend in this book, is to be viewed as one element in a triangulated set of feminine archetypes (mother, whore, and asexual celibate), the spinster's disappearance signals underlying shifts in the meaning assigned the icon. The emergence of new ideas about women in relation to family, sexuality, and work have produced new mythologies and stereotypes to support those views. Therefore, while real women sometimes appear in this narrative, it is their fictionalized rather than their actual selves that are germane to the story I have to tell.

The spinster is hardly unique in the annals of our cultural history. Other women (and men, as well) have occupied similarly significant positions. Pocahontas and Cinderella, for example, are perennial favorites among purveyors of popular culture and one could easily compile a whole catalogue of cultural types, including the "mammy" and the "stepmother," that have been used as stock characters to round out the plots and fill the gaps in cultural productions. Neither, as Robert Tilton persuasively argued in his book about the changing portrayal of Pocahontas over the past three centuries, are the representations of such figures constant. The almost mythic individuals that come to inhabit a culture's imagination across successive generations, or what has been called the "longue duree," are recurrent precisely because they "express multiple and at times contradictory agendas."[9]

Cultural icons are like the standardized representations of religious figures that were prominent in medieval times, conventionally rendered representations of stock images. They are not just cultural incidentals; rather, they provide what social theoretician Erving Goffman called "frames," those "schemata of interpretation" that enable individuals to define, categorize, and explain experience. By "rendering what would otherwise be a meaningless aspect of the scene into something that is meaningful," they function as templates for determining "what is going on here," for "making sense," and for "organizing experience."[10] Like other cultural reference points such as standard metaphors and stereotypes, they are frequently employed because their lineaments are understood to be well defined. They are, as historian Alan Trachtenberg cogently observed, "of prime historical interest" because, as "vehicles of self-knowledge" and "concepts upon which people act," they are "forces in their own right." Along with material and political factors, they affect both perceptions and behavior.[11]

However, as with the ever-popular but dramatically changing vampire chronicled by Nina Auerbach in *Our Vampires Ourselves*, both fictional and fictionalized icons also mirror changes in the society that produces them and, consequently, their representational elements are likely to change dramatically over time. Conversely, when the larger-than-life personages, such as the raccoon-skin-hatted Davy Crockett, can no longer be reshaped in accordance with the ideological requirements of the time, they become expendable. Cultural icons are jettisoned only when they can no longer be redesigned and reclothed in conformity with contemporary needs, preoccupations, and tastes.

Of course, there were flesh and blood women who were called spinsters and who thought of themselves in those terms, but I think that embodiment was not, perhaps, of as much historical moment as the existence of the idea. It was the cultural inscriptions that defined the female bachelor; the fantasized nature of such a person, more than the actual behavior of any real persons had direct consequences for women's life chances. In the discussion that follows, I will concentrate on the changing perceptions of spinsterhood—the factors that facilitated the transformation of spinsters into exemplars of female accomplishment, the circumstances in which they came to lose that role, and the consequences of that transition.

For these reasons, the best place to search for the causes of the initial rise, the complex evolution, and the eventual banishment of positive images of spinsters from popular imagination is in the realms they inhabited—the magazines, books, and movies that propagated those images.

In the United States, definitions and disputes about what it means to be a woman and how to be a woman have been inscribed in, conveyed through, and countered in the mass media for at least a century. Therefore, in my search for clues as to the reasons for the spinster's prominence and the occasion of her demise, I looked for the old maid's most public face in media that had achieved widespread distribution. In particular, I looked at three kinds of material: the *Ladies' Home Journal*, a magazine that began publication in December 1883 and was the most widely read of the women's magazines for some decades;[12] mass-market books that aimed at explicating the psychology of women; and high-grossing movies made in the United States after 1930.

These sources, all of which successfully targeted mass audiences, constituted central forums for the popular representation of and discussion of gender issues. The *Ladies' Home Journal*, one of the earliest, most successful, and longest-lived of the women's magazines, provides an abundance of images of spinsterhood through the 1930s. In the 1920s and 1930s, the doctrines of the emerging psychological establishment facilitated the development of a new set of understandings of spinsterhood, promulgating a sexual understanding of that condition. In the following decade, Hollywood films, the preeminent media from the Depression onward, presented increasingly negative depictions of spinsters even though higher and higher proportions of women were marrying and doing so at a younger age. Taken together, these sources document an intriguing trajectory of concerns about women.

The *Ladies' Home Journal* is a rich vein of information about mainstream views on women for the years between 1884 (when its second issue appeared) and the beginning of World War I. Both its content and its pronouncements were of some consequence to the public; by century's end it had become one of the most influential of the publications designed to reach women. Describing the early trajectory of the magazine in her book, *Magazines for the Millions*, Helen Damon-Moore notes that even though an audience for women's magazines was already well established, the *Journal's* publisher broke new ground in the mass-circulation market. He used paid advertisements to subsidize the price of the magazine, offering premiums for new subscriptions and included an attractive compilation of short stories, features, and domestic departments. In consequence, its circulation reached 25,000 at the end of one year, doubled during the next six months, and reached 400,000 in 1886.[13]

The materials produced by "experts" in the fields of sexology and psychoanalysis and disseminated in the popular press also proved of some value in this inquiry. After World War I, popularized versions of psychoanalytic theory reached a wide public not only through best-selling books such as Farnham and Lundberg's *Modern Woman*[14] or Van de Velde's *Ideal Marriage*,[15] but also through school texts and countless numbers of magazine and newspaper articles.

Finally, to complete the trajectory of images, I consider the presentations of spinsterhood in movies, especially in those films made after the rise of the studio system and the development of a national distribution system in the 1930s. A number of spinsters appeared in Hollywood films in this period and, almost inevitably, the movie plot explored both the causes and the consequences of their single status. Those tales, which integrated and reflected on the pronouncements of psychologists and psychoanalysts, are significant for their discussions about gender and the cultural construction of "normal femininity."

The clues both to the spinster's persistence and eventual disappearance linger in popular culture, which is both vehicle and medium of standardized imagery. In the twentieth century the apparatus of mass culture has become a center for popular representations. As such it contains what one sociologist described as the "texts that mediate [people's] . . . sense of themselves and their social world[,]" and therefore investigation of such texts allows for "analysis of the arrangements through which a social order is reconstituted."[16]

I am not suggesting that consumers of mass culture such as magazine readers or moviegoers were or are cultural dopes, nor do I think that the mere presentation of gender prescriptions in magazines and movies is sufficient to produce emulative behavior. Rather, I would argue, the standardized representations of women in popular culture, whether authoritative or mundane, both affected and reflected views on the character and nature of womanhood. As literary critic Jen Ang said, the pleasure taken in the fictions produced in mass media does not necessarily "imply that we are also bound to take up their positions and solutions in our relations to our loved ones and friends, our work, our political ideals, and so on."[17] "Texts," as opposed to "scripts"—cultural products that succeed in the mass market—"mediate" practice.[18] In this way popular culture both accepts dominant assumptions and struggles over their meaning. It is possible then to locate not only dominant ideas (as opposed to practices) but also areas of general cultural uneasiness in widely disseminated and consumed cultural products. This is certainly the case for the spinster.

Although the term "spinster" has a long pedigree, spinsters did not come to play an important role in the public imagination until the eighteenth century. According to the *Oxford English Dictionary* (*OED*), it literally means a person who spins, probably reflecting a task that once belonged to unmarried women.[19] By the seventeenth century, however, the term had become "the proper legal designation" for women "still unmarried," no matter what their age or eventual marital intentions. Thus, one commonly finds the formula, "a spinster of this parish," in funeral as well as wedding announcements of old.

It was not until the eighteenth century that the term "spinster" became synonymous with the equally ancient, but considerably less-neutral appellation, "old maid." The "old maid" was not only an "unmarried" woman, but also one "beyond the usual age for marriage," and the term, the authoritative *OED* makes clear, was used in such a way as to connote the sometimes foolish "habits characteristic of such a condition."[20] Such aged maidens were, in fact, common figures in fiction produced for the American literary market, and they came in for a fair amount of derision. It is not my purpose to speculate on the reasons for such ridicule, but it might have stemmed from the conjunction of the two words "old" and "maid," calling up simultaneous images of the "trappings and infirmities" of advanced age and the presumably innocent status of maidenhood and its employments.

In any case, thereafter spinsters seem to have acted as defining images for gender construction for a substantial period of time. Most notably, for a century after the Civil War, the "old maid" figured for each generation as the embodiment of the woman who was "not" married but still respectable and, in that context, as an alternative form of womanhood. This positioning was not, of course, limited to the United States. In her history of single women in Victorian Britain, Martha Vicinus argues that a triangle of mythic possibilities existed for women. In this period, she says, "a woman . . . was either the ideal mother/wife or a celibate spinster or a promiscuous prostitute." Such was also the case on this side of the Atlantic.[21]

In the United States, as in Britain, proscriptive and prescriptive constructions in the popular media identified the never-marrying woman as the modal category of "un"married propriety. Even though she had never entered the expected estate for adult women—that of marriage. In the logic of the time, she was, by definition, a "maiden"; that is, she was presumed to have remained sexually inactive and, accordingly, in possession of her maidenhead. In an age when premarital sexual activity was the sine qua non of female delinquency, celibacy was both a marker and a (presumed) consequence of decency. And, if single women who were celibate were respectable, mutatus mutandi, single women who were respectable were assumed to be sexually inactive (needless to say, so long as disconfirming evidence didn't turn up).

Conversely, this understanding fed an assumption that underlay commentary from the twentieth as well as the nineteenth century, namely, that "real" spinsters were chaste and celibate and thus, by definition, that the spinster was respectable. Of course, that was a big assumption. Although we know a fair amount about the proportions of women who remained single in each generation, we know actually very little about their erotic lives.[22] There is a dearth of evidence about female sexual practice in the late nineteenth and early twentieth centuries, and historians who have investigated women's sexuality during this period disagree both about the character of women's desire and the nature of their erotic activities.[23]

It is also true that real spinsters came from a broad range of educational, geographic, ethnic, and class backgrounds and were likely quite varied in skin tones. My own aunt, for example, came from a family that was far from elite. My grandparents, Russian Jews who came to the United States in 1910 when my aunt was four years old never did much more than eke out a living, he as a peddler and she as a seamstress. Or again, Sarah and Elizabeth Delaney, the rather more successful African-American women whose best-selling 1993 autobiography, *Having Our Say: The Delaney Sisters' First One Hundred Years*, was turned into a successful play, describe themselves as preferring to remain single. Yet as the following chapters make clear, in popular iconography, the unmarried woman was almost always represented as well educated, white, and of privileged background. This rendering not only set the spinster apart from the mass; her mere appearance facilitated a set of implicit comparisons to women who were habitually designated as "inferiors." In fact, I would argue, it was precisely because the spinster was always portrayed as a woman of the "superior" sort that her one deviation from the ideal—the fact that she was unattached—came to define her as a key figure in an evolving series of debates about womanhood.

Still, the designation "spinster" had concrete as well as ideological referents. The demographic record indicates that from the time of the American Revolution until the 1920s, approximately eight of one hundred American women remained single for life. More consequentially, between the Civil War and World War I, in some regions of the United States, there were especially large cohorts of women who never married.[24] The causal factors that sustained low marriage rates for women are not clear. However, in the latter part of the nineteenth century, there was an "excess" of marriageable women, especially in the Northeast. This sexual imbalance has been linked to a variety of factors, including high male death rates in the Civil War, the migration westward of men from unproductive farmland in the East, and a propensity toward delayed marriage among the native born.[25]

In addition, however, there is good evidence that some nineteenth-century women actively chose to remain unwed, rejecting what many recognized as the burdens imposed by a lifetime commitment to a man, the concomitant risks of childbearing and the rigors of motherhood.[26] Lee Chambers-Schiller argues that as women emerged as an intellectual and literary force in the first half of the nineteenth century, independence was increasingly adduced as an inherent attribute of the situation of unmarried women. In an analysis of the diaries, letters, memoirs, and other writings of a group of notable women, Chambers-Schiller found substantial evidence for the emergence of what she refers to as a "cult of single blessedness" among the generations of 1780 to 1840. Based on this evidence, she contends that in the half century after the Revolution, increasing numbers of women "upheld the single life as both a socially and personally valuable state" and, through the choice against marriage, "articulated the values of female independence."

This new attitude stood in contrast to those of previous generations. Seventeenth-century New Englanders, she says, "deemed singlehood a sinful state, an evil to be exorcised from community life because solitary women menaced the social order." Single women were a problem because they imperiled family life, not because of their personal shortcomings. It was not until the eighteenth century, she argues, that writers began to emphasize the "peculiar personality defects and particular character foibles" of unmarried women. But, even then, the descriptions of spinsters rendered them infantile rather than bizarre. Writers of the period, she says, emphasized their "unsurpassed curiosity, childlike credulity, absurd affectations and spiteful natures," as well as their "intolerable peevishness, envy of the young, aversion to the old, . . . insatiable avidity of conquest, and hopeless aspirations after matrimony."

A new idea emerged for the generations of women born between 1780 and 1840, according to Chambers-Schiller. For increasing numbers of these women, remaining single was a way to reject "the self-abnegation inherent in domesticity" in order to engage in the "cultivation of the self." In the words and ideas of republicanism, Chambers-Schiller argues, women found the metaphors for a cultural reassessment of singlehood as a form of independence and a critique of marriage and domesticity.[27] The increasing number of publications by such women is testimony to the power of these ideas.

My investigation began where Chambers-Schiller's ended, at the fin de siècle. In these years, as a result of access to higher education, spinsterhood was increasingly associated with feminine independence. Only the unmarried woman was deemed able to pursue a career and live alone. In fact, in this period, unmarried women may well have been the prime beneficiaries of expanding opportunities for women. At the birth of the Republic, women had few civil rights and only limited avenues of independent action. During the course of the next century they achieved recognition as legal persons, gained control over their own property, entered into arenas formerly closed to them, and even though they lacked the franchise, emerged as a force in public life. But the women best positioned to enjoy the fruits of these changes were those least encumbered by domestic responsibilities and, perhaps for that reason, it was the unmarried woman who stood in the public mind as the prime exemplar of feminine freedom.

As Chambers-Schiller has documented, women who eschewed marriage pronounced themselves free during the heady years after American independence. Yet even in the wake of the victories of the early movement for woman's rights, intellectual independence did not guarantee economic self-sufficiency. Not until the turn of the century could single women live alone. With access to higher education and to professional careers, they came into their own both literally and figuratively. In fact, social and vocational opportunities for unmarried college women expanded so rapidly that by the turn of the twentieth century the spinster came to be seen, in the mass media at least, as one of the happiest as well as most self-sufficient of her sex.

The spinster's post-World War I successor was not so lucky. Still regarded as successful in worldly terms, she was increasingly represented as sexually repressed and emotionally bereft. But this was not the nadir of her existence. During and after World War II, despite her rapidly decreasing representation in the population, the never-marrying, celibate woman was presented to mass audiences as an exemplar of feminine failure. This book looks at how those transformations were accomplished and what they implied.

Initially, I undertook the task of unraveling the spinster's demise as a way of explicating the forces that made her culturally irrelevant. What I came to appreciate, however, was that for several generations of women, she represented an "alternative" feminine path and, as such, participated in the expansion and contraction of gendered possibilities. Perhaps in consequence, she occupied a prominent place in American imagery long after the sexual climate that elevated and sustained her had been utterly transformed. In fact, I argue, for a number of generations of Americans, the old maid was both sign and symbol of a certain order of womanhood that served as a cultural resource, a representative type who could be invoked to interpret and explain or guide and rebuke. Therefore, the character of spinster portraiture reveals as much about attitudes toward women in general as it does about views of "old maids," and changes in spinster imagery are indicative of alterations in concerns about women.

It seems most appropriate to use fiction for the analysis of a fiction, and for that reason I center the spinster's tale on three short stories that appeared in the *Ladies' Home Journal* in 1890, 1913, and 1933. These pieces caught my attention as I scrolled through microfilm copies of the magazine for selected years; when I began to put this manuscript together they came to seem more and more crucial to the history I was describing.[28] However, I found it impossible to write about them; no mere summary could do them justice. Therefore, I decided to reprint them in all their glorious totality, and they appear in chapters two, four, and six. In the first, "Rebekah Spofford's Theory," written in 1890, *Journal* regular Emma Hewitt followed a plucky and determined college graduate who temporarily devoted herself to saving the family farm but never wavered from her double commitment to career and spinsterhood. Rebekah's 1913 successor in "The Woman Who Threw Herself Away" was far less determined. In this Christmas fable, freelance author Margarita Spalding Gerry induced an attractive young college professor, Miss Metcalf, and her equally attractive and even younger undergraduate acolyte, Helen Standish, to rethink their intention of remaining single. Taking them on a visit to the home of a former college servant, she provided them with a timely reminder of the blessings of maternity. In the last of the stories, written twenty years later, Mary Carolyn (whose last name is mentioned only twice in passing by author Lois Montross) contemplated giving up marriage for a career for a brief time. But an encounter with the perversions of academia was sufficient to bring her first to her senses and then to marriage.

All three stories seem very peculiar to me and I am not alone in this view. After the first reader of this manuscript, historian Nancy Tomes, had gone through them, we had a short debate about which was the most bizarre and found that we could make a good case for giving the award to each one. It is, I would contend, their very oddity that kept me thinking about them and commends them as historically useful documents. They are certainly not, as I am sure the readers of this book will agree, literary masterpieces. But as they were published in the *Journal,* they must have met both the magazine's standards for content and presentation. The very representations that appear odd to the modern reader must have seemed reasonable to the editorial staff and, presumably, its audience. For these reasons, even though they were unique creations, they also drew on general anxieties and concerns and purveyed what were, at least for the times, accepted truths. Therefore, although I neither present these tales as a random sample of fictions produced at the time nor claim them as "typical" in any way, it seems obvious that the portraits of spinsterhood they offer were accepted variants of the genre.

The fact that the heroines of these stories were all college women is not accidental. For quite a long period of time, education was considered as much a prerequisite for women intent on professional careers as spinsterhood was its consequence. Indeed, Barbara Solomon suggests that in the United States before World War I, many of the women who went to college aiming at a career were reacting to, or resolved upon, spinsterhood.[29] The assumption of an interrelationship among higher education, careers for women, and marriage refusal was most pronounced at the turn of the century, but the possibility that advanced degrees might suffice to draw a woman away from marriage persisted as an undercurrent for several generations of writers. As a result, popular culture often cut the garments of spinsterhood to fit the figure of the "college girl" and then paraded her as modeling virtue, vice, or something in between.

Even though female collegians were still relatively uncommon in the United States at the turn of the century,[30] they attracted considerable attention. The flower of American womanhood, they were frequent subjects of debate in both scholarly and popular domains. College education, the desire for a professional career, and a propensity to avoid marriage were implicitly linked in many of the pieces published in the *Ladies' Home Journal* during its first half century. The assumption that the three were associated was most pronounced at the turn of the century, but the possibility that advanced degrees might suffice to draw a woman away from the path toward marriage persisted as an undercurrent for several generations of writers, even as they urged women to prepare for domestic life.

Until the 1940s, when the *Journal* began to limit its focus more definitively to women already married and their accompanying domestic requirements, the image of college "girls" graced the pages of the magazine with some frequency.[31] Editorials discussed them, features elicited their opinions, fashion pieces celebrated their style, and stories described their particular dilemmas.

Although the plots of the stories reprinted here are unique, they share a series of common elements. As college women, the heroines inhabit a realm of preparation. In addition, all three stories place young women in unsettling situations that both provide valuable life lessons and aid them in fixing on their future course. In that situation, each story requires that its heroine contemplate and select either marriage or career—which are presented as mutually exclusive life alternatives. Suggestively, however, neither love nor romance is described as a significant element in the decision to marry or remain single. In fact, these characters are portrayed as either uninterested in marriage or willing to give up the idea of wedlock for something better.[32] These pieces inevitably included reflexive comparisons between the married and unmarried states in which the former is depicted, at best, as the lesser of two evils.

The writers who delivered these stories were obviously well regarded, but they were not authorial stars, and their contributions would have, in all likelihood, run the gauntlet of editorial review with its attendant requirements. Not the production of well-known authors who commanded large sums for work not yet written, the young women who inhabited these tales may have been individual creations who embodied their creators' peculiarities, but they must also have passed some tests of resonance and been deemed appropriate for the magazine. Moreover, as all three stories were written by women who had been married at least once, they were equally unlikely to reflect the spinster's viewpoint.

Designed to entertain, the three stories reveal much about contemporary perceptions of the attractions, dilemmas, and possibilities available to women within collegiate precincts. As one historian points out, the *Journal* was self-consciously prescriptive.[33] But the magazine did not create cultural standards; rather, it functioned as a conduit for the repetition and reinforcement of ideas and axioms that reflected mainstream beliefs. Therefore, while it is certainly not the case that its advice was always accepted by or even acceptable to its readers, the *Journal's* contents certainly reflected and were resonant with widely held views of the time. Indeed, it is precisely because of their thematic unity that these stories can be read as indicating constant elements as well as shifts in attitudes toward women, particularly well-educated women. What the authors made of such predilections is especially telling.

No account of popular culture in the twentieth century would be complete without a discussion of film. So I conclude the spinster's tale by examining her representation in a number of successful cinematic productions, most notably, *Now, Voyager* (1942) and *Summertime* (1955). It is my contention that the spinster portrayals that are so central to these movies reflected a transition in attitudes about dangers to the social fabric that simultaneously limited women's options and facilitated the emergence of a movement for their liberation.

Cinema stories not only reflected popular perceptions of women; they were also central to the process of (en)gendering ideas and concerns about the family. As a medium that consistently reached a wider national audience than any that had preceded it, films both echoed existing stereotypes and created new ways of seeing. For Graeme Turner, movies inform us not only about the "systems" but also about the "processes" of culture both as "product *and* social practice."[34] Like other "works of imagination," they are what Elizabeth Cowrie pungently described as "part of our negotiation of 'sour reality.' "[35] "The ideological interchange between film and culture," Robert Kolker notes, operates through a complex system and therefore

> [t]he images and narratives of women that filmmakers create must be shared by both sexes in order to exist. If audiences did not assent to the images, they would not go to see them; if they were not seen, they would no longer be made. That they were made and continue to be made . . . indicates either that the producers 'cliche'—"we give the public what it wants"—is true, or that the "public" accepts whatever it is given and in that acceptance is molded into a state of assent.[36]

Perhaps for this reason, the analysis of Hollywood films has proved especially attractive to theoreticians of gender.[37]

As you will see, both the *Journal* and Hollywood used spinster imagery as a way of addressing the basic desires, character, and potential of American womanhood. However, the spinsterhood plotlines devised by mass media authors changed over time, suggesting alterations in what was thought best for the most excellent of the nation's young women. Most significantly, changes in the way this subject was approached describe not only transitions in attitudes toward the single life and its practitioners but also about the constituent elements of "normal" femininity, reflecting a trajectory in attitudes about what is characteristic or "natural" for women in general and educated women in particular.

TWO

"BOSSED BY A WOMAN"

THE FIRST OF THE college-girl stories, "Rebekah Spofford's Theory,"[1] was published in September 1890. Written by Emma Hewitt, a *Journal* regular who had been brought onto the staff in 1886 by the magazine's first editor, Louisa Knapp,[2] it approvingly depicted a college-educated woman who chose career over family. Occupying only two-and-a-half of the magazine's large-sized pages, it was accompanied by pen-and-ink renderings presumably meant to evoke images of rural life. Only one drawing included the story's heroine. It depicted a woman on horseback talking to a man on foot. The woman's features are indistinct, however, establishing a distance

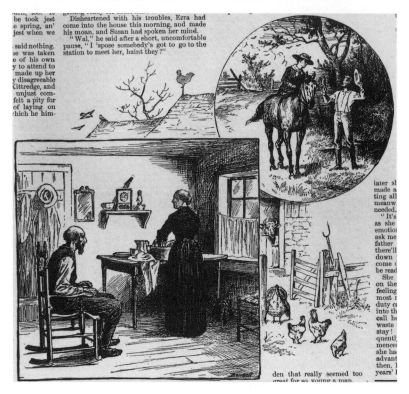

between Rebekah and the reader that is echoed by the story's beginning, the words of a man in distress.

REBEKAH SPOFFORD'S THEORY

by Emma C. Hewitt, 1902

Farmer Kittredge sat rocking himself slowly back and forth. Susan, his wife was equally silent, but vented her agitation, whatever it might be, in the more woman-like way of increased occupation, and washed dishes and poked the fire with added vigor.

Farmer Kittredge groaned. Then he burst forth into fretful complaining.

"Massy! Massy!" he wailed. "It's awful hard at my age to be so put to it! They's no use talkin'. Things can't go on an' in six months the mor'gidge'll be foreclosed because I haint the money to settle with. It seems as if the hand of Providence was dretful heavy." He paused a moment and passed his hand over his pale, blue eyes and weak mouth.

"There's that sickness o' yourn, too. It was very hard that you sh'd be took jest while we was a-plantin' in the spring, an hefto hev a help in the kitchen jest when we needed every cent."

Susan Kittredge bit her lip, but said nothing. She might have retorted that she was taken sick from overwork at the time of his own sickness and consequent inability to attend to his legitimate duties. She had made up her mind long ago, however, to many disagreeable things in the make-up of Ezra Kittredge, and his complaining injustice (or unjust complaints) was one of them. She felt a pity for this man, who was so fond of laying on Providence many of the evils which he himself might have averted had he had the character or disposition. She felt in her instinctive womanly way that this man was handicapped by nature, and that, such as he was, she had married him for better, for worse—that it had proved *worse*, instead of *better*, was her misfortune. Besides, too, she took consolation in the fact that his short-comings were weaknesses, not wickednesses. As for that, he might have been much "worse" than he was. So she had bravely tried all these years to supplement his short-comings, having long ago learned that it is almost impossible to *guide* a weak man.

"There's Becky, too," he broke out again, fretfully. "That fool trick of hers, goin' away to get a college education! Just 's if we weren't good enough for her here! That money o' hern, ef it hed ben put into the farm might 'a' saved it. But no! She must go edicate herself all to nothin,' an she'll come back so sassy and stuck-up there'll be no livin' with her, like's not. Ef she'd 'a' been a *boy*, she'd a stuck by the old farm."

"I don't think even *boys* 'stick by the old farm' always," answered his wife significantly.

Ezra shuffled his feet uneasily. He didn't like the way his wife had of remembering things, and bringing them up to him, and it was specially unpleasant just now that she should remember the time when he ran away from home. He had in him the desire to do something and strike out for himself, but his natural weakness of character had interfered, so he had only run to another farm a few miles away.

"Ezra," said Susan, firmly, "we may as well understand each other. I won't have Becky interfered with. The money was her own, an' 'ef she wanted the education,' she's welcome to it. Lord knows life on a farm isn't so pleasant that she need want to stay on one! Now let this be the last. I'm glad she' got learnin' so she can teach and do something besides dig, dig, dig all day long an' half the night, too, for that matter. An' let me tell you *another* thing, Ezra Kittredge, ef Becky had ben a *boy*, stead of a girl, ef I could 'a' helped it, she never should 'a' put one cent of that money into this farm."

Ezra Kittredge was assailed by two emotions upon being the recipient of this address—fear and astonishment. Seldom, indeed was it that long-suffering Susan Kittredge "spoke her mind," but when she did, Ezra Kittredge "feared" and was silent. He respected whatever wishes she might be pleased to express in that tone.

So Becky Spofford and her money, were henceforth tabooed as topics of conversation.

And what of Becky herself? Rebekah Spofford had, some ten years before, been astonished to learn that her widowed mother was about to marry Ezra Kittredge. But, being her mother's own daughter, she had asked no questions, accepting, in her own way, the inevitable. Her surprise at her mother's move, however, had never ceased, and, at twenty-one, coming in possession of her little inheritance she had taken a thousand dollars of it in her hand and had gone away to a distant city to obtain the "edication" before alluded to.

In the two years intervening between her departure and the present time matters at the farm had gone anything but well. "The hand of Providence," according to Farmer Kittredge, had fallen heavily on him several times, and he seemed, each time, less able to recuperate after the blow. The neighbors did not share his faith in the chastening "hand of Providence," but they were a conservative community, and had not yet felt called upon to tell neighbor Kittredge that many of his afflictions arose from his obstinate mismanagement, or from lack of management altogether, upon his part. *They* knew that when his young corn was devoured by straying cows, it was because his fences had not yet been attended to; but then that was *his* affair, not theirs.

Now, the affliction seemed to be that the cattle were feverish and miserable, and evidently getting ready for some kind of a sickness.

Disheartened with his troubles, Ezra had come into the house this morning and made his moan, and Susan had spoken her mind.

"Wal," he said after a short, uncomfortable pause, "I 'spose somebody's got to go to the station to meet her, haint they?"

"Certainly," answered his wife, decidedly. "The idea! Rebekah, after an absence of two years being obliged to *walk* from the station, two miles away!"

"Wal—I didn't just know. She *used* to be *fond* o' walkin', an' I thought mebbe, as the horses was busy harvestin'—"

"She'll not walk *this* time," broke in his wife with a promptness and decision that at once put to flight any notions Ezra might have had in relation to persuading her that Rebekah might as well walk.

"Wal," he said slowly, as he passed out of the house. So decided had been his wife's reply, that Ezra did not wait even to be told, but had the small wagon at the door exactly at three o'clock. He knew he would not be called upon to drive, but he hung around till Susan was fairly off, anxious in some way to propitiate his wife, with whom he felt, in an undefined way, that he was in disgrace. Everything about Ezra Kittredge *was* undefined. Still, he felt that the root of the present uncomfortable feeling lay in the fact that he had proposed that Rebekah should walk, and he was anxious to do everything in his power towards enabling her to ride, and thus, in some measure propitiate his wife.

"O mother!" exclaimed Rebekah, as she threw her arms around the form so dear to her, "it has been a hard, sweet, long, short, two years!" and the tears stood in her eyes, as contradictory of the smile upon her lips as were her words of each other.

Susan Kittredge, I have said, was a silent woman, so she only pressed her daughter to her heart, while the tears stood in her eyes, and her lips trembled with pent-up emotion.

"Tell me, dear," she said in a tender tone, "all about yourself, Becky. Letters is so unsatisfyin'."

Rebekah felt as if some one had struck her a blow. Surely her mother had degenerated since she went away! Or was it merely that two years' absence had not only made her forgetful of her mother's defects, but more sensitive and alive to them? Still, she could forgive many lapses in the mother she loved so well. She hid her disappointment under a lively chatter as to her doings in all the time she had been away.

The mother said little, more than content to listen to the recital, so that Rebekah was hardly prepared for things as she found them when she arrived at "Asparagus Cottage," by which unromantic name her home had been known (no one could tell wherefore) for the last fifty years. The gates were loose, fences were rickety, the steps broken, and there was a general air of unthrift, that Rebekah noticed at once, with a combination of dismay and rejoicing—rejoicing, that in the autumn she would go away again to teach; dismay, that all her summer must be spent in such surroundings.

Still, it would be life in the country, and she had so longed, all these months, for a breath of the old home—a touch of nature as she had known her since she was first rocked in one of Nature's own cradles, the grand, old elms that stood beside the door-post. These, at least, were unchanged, and as Rebekah went to her room and gazed out upon the well-remembered landscape, noting all the familiar points, then came over her a feeling of content. She could not help noting, however, that prosperity was all round them— "Asparagus Cottage" alone looked as if the years had not been kind to it.

When Farmer Kittredge came in to supper, Rebekah noted also, that the old look of deprecation and discontent was more marked, and that time had laid a heavy finger on her step-father making premature lines and seams, and pressing down his shoulders with a burden that really seemed too great for so young a man.

"Wal, Becky," said he, after the dishes were washed and they sat down for a few moments quiet before the early retiring, "I 'spose you're awful smart."

Rebekah laughed, while she inwardly wondered why her step-father's lapses of speech did not disturb her, as did those of her mother. She had not yet learned that we would have *perfect* those we love. The faults and failing of those for whom we have no affection, do not disturb our peace of mind.

"Well, no! I do not know that I'm 'awful smart', as you call it, but I *do* know that I have put in two years' hard work, and that I have made them tell." She spoke with the consciousness of work well done and time well spent.

"What ye goin' to do *now*," queried Farmer Kittredge, with an anxiety in his tone that each woman noted but interpreted differently.

"I am going to teach in the fall," answered Rebekah, adding a moment after—in a tone which showed plainly what *her* interpretation had been— "I shall not be here after the first of September, and a part of August I am going to visit a school friend at the shore."

She watched her step-father as she spoke, and marveled a little that there did not appear on his face that sense of relief which she expected would follow her announcement. Her mother said nothing, and as there seemed to be a great dearth of conversation, the family went to their respective rooms.

Matters went on quietly for a day or two, Rebekah renewing her acquaintance with old nooks and corners, and taking a hand in all kinds of work much to her mother's distress, for she considered that her daughter should take a rest.

"Never mind *me*, mother dear. Don't you know that home-work is a rest for brain workers? Scientists tell us that change of occupation is real rest; so you see no one need be idle at any time, and you don't know how I've *longed*, a hundred times, to have my hands in the bread-dough or to iron my own clothes. I must confess, however" she added, laughing, "that I've never seen the time when I longed to churn or have anything to do with butter-making. You know I always did *hate* that. I suppose you use the same old churn?"

"Yes, I'm awful glad, Becky. D'ye know I was so 'fraid that ye'd got to be so smart, an' all that, y'd hate our ways an' the work an' all," and the poor woman's eyes filled with tears of relief. "An' Ezra, he—" but one of those crises had arrived which take us all so unawares sometimes, and the mother, utterly to her own surprise, and the consternation of her daughter, flung herself down in her chair and burst into tears.

Rebekah had never seen her mother shed a tear since the day she laid John Spofford away to rest in the little churchyard out on the hill, and she was stunned by this exhibition of grief. She waited a few moments until the storm had spent itself, and then laying her hand tenderly on her mother's head, as if their places had been reversed, said softly, "Tell me all about it, mother dear, and let us see if it can be helped." The gentle touch and the tender words, started the tears again, but this time they fell quietly, and after a little, with a sobbing sigh, Mrs. Kittredge wiped her eyes and the storm was over.

"Now, mother, tell me," commanded Rebekah again as she softly stroked the hair, grown so white during her two year's absence. And then, such is human nature, the mother, without a word of apology, told her daughter everything of which she had so firmly forbidden her husband to speak. "And now," she added, with another gasping sob that threatened a re-opening of the storm, "you're goin' away agin in the fall, an' I reely don't know what I *shall* do 'thout you, an everything goin' to rack an' ruin so!"

"Don't cry any more, mother," said Rebekah, in a tone from which all the life had gone, "it hurts me so to see you like that. Let me think awhile and I'll see what we can do. There, mother," she added with a tender little pat, "don't let things worry you. It will all come out right, I feel sure; but I must go away and think for myself." And with a kiss, she went away for self-communion, leaving the poor woman comforted. Becky had said things would be all right, and she must know of course, since she had been two years learning it all.

The force of years of habit led Rebekah up to the hay-loft, and here, the door flung open, gazing out on the fair fields stretched out before her, she thought out the problem, as she had done many another in the girl-life that now seemed so far behind her. An hour later she came down from her eyrie, and made a slow tour of the farm, mentally noting all she saw, and making calculations meanwhile as to waste, thrift and money needed.

"It's all right, mother," she said quietly, as she came in pale and tired with the emotions of the past two hours; "but don't ask me about it until I am ready to speak. If father Kittredge don't act out, I don't think there'll be any trouble. But I must go lie down now. I don't want any dinner. I'll come down to supper and by that time I'll be ready to speak to father Kittredge."

She went slowly up stairs, threw herself on the bed and then relieved her pent up feelings by a flood of tears. It seemed almost more than she could bear! *Did* her duty call her to stay *here,* instead of entering into the work her soul loved? Did her duty call her to put herself into this work and waste the study of the past two years? But stay! Waste? Had she herself not eloquently told the listening public on Commencement-day, that such an education as she had received was a preparation and an advantage in *any* walk of life? Could she then, legitimately call it *wasted*—her two years' hard work?

But it was *hard!* She pled with her soul. Hard? Certainly; but then she would have an opportunity of showing father Kittredge, and a few other doubters, that her higher education had only made her more competent instead of spoiling her.

The sacrifice assumed entirely new proportions in her sight, when viewed in this light, and with a grave determination to do her best, she put aside all personal feelings in the matter, and began to lay plans for her future work.

"Father Kittredge," said she after supper (she always called him 'Father Kittredge' out of respect to her mother, though, out of respect to herself, she had never brought her mind to place him in her dead father's place by addressing him simply as "father").

"Wal?"

"I had a little talk with mother to-day, and she tells me things haven't gone well with you," said Rebekah, kindly.

She had made up her mind that if she undertook this thing, for her own comfort's sake, she must overlook the faults and failings of the people with whom she was going to live.

"I sh'd say they hain't. The hand o' Providence has been laid might heavy on me. There's Mollie, the very best Alderney of the lot, jist a dyin'. An' they all seem to be sickenin'."

The "hand o' Providence" was the thing with which Rebekah had the least patience, but she controlled the hasty words that rose to her lips and said, "Are any one's else [sic] cattle sick in the neighborhood?"

"No, on'y mine. I tell you its the hand o' Providence, and there don't seem to be no use fightin' it."

Seeing that there was no progress to be made in this direction, Rebekah concluded to come at once to the point.

"Well now, I have a plan to propose. You say that the hand of Providence is against you, and that all things work wrong with you. I have a little money, you know (Farmer Kittredge's eyes brightened), which I am willing to put into the farm, but on conditions."

The hope that had been in Ezra's face became anxiety.

"My conditions are that for one year you shall give up the farm into my hands altogether. Matters surely cannot go worse with me than they have with you. If I do what I hope to do, the money can be paid back later on, and meanwhile, I ask no interest for its use. If I undertake it, I shall submit to no dictation. I shall ask advice when I think I need it. Unless I *do* ask it, I don't expect to have it offered to me. It will only hamper and irritate me. My ways will not be your ways, that I know before I begin, and, to avoid all misunderstanding, I make this plain statement which I shall firmly adhere to."

To say that father Kittredge was surprised would but mildly express his condition of mind.

"I don't know's I care to give my work up into a woman's han's," he said aggressively, after he had thought awhile.

"Very well," replied Rebekah, quietly, "you know best, of course, how your affairs stand, and what you want to do. You can take till to-morrow to think of it; if you change your mind by that time let me know. But I must make other arrangements soon, and I must know at once. Besides, if I take things in charge, I should like to begin in time to save the lives of the cattle, who will all die under present arrangements. When thinking over this, remember that I am no ignorant girl attempting work of which she knows nothing, but a girl who has been born and bred on a farm, and who can bring to her work the added assistance of higher education, scientifically applied. Good night."

It will never be known as to just what methods of persuasion or intimidation were used by Susan Kittredge to accomplish her end, but it is a fact that the next morning, father Kittredge gave his consent, in the most lugubrious manner, to her taking charge of the farm for one year on the conditions named. His funereal tone she chose to ignore, but accepted the charge at once.

"Father Kittredge," she said after all details were settled, "there's just one thing I want to speak about. I prefer to be called Rebekah and not 'Becky.' Please try to remember."

"Massy! Massy! I *said* she'd come home sassy," groaned he to himself. "Takes the farm out 'o my hands 'cause I can't help myself, an' then wants to be called 'Rebekah.' 'Rebekah,' he repeated in a mimicing tone to himself. "Wall, we'll see," he added consolingly. "Jest wait tell the hand 'o Providence is laid on *her*, an' *then* where'll she be?"

There were no legal documents—merely a note of the bargain made out in Rebekah's clear hand, and signed by all three parties to the transaction.

"And now, father Kittredge, will you see that Silas takes the cattle over to the south pasture, instead of the north lot. I am perfectly convinced that there is some pollution in the water of that brook, and, until I have time to have it examined, I prefer to try the change." So much against his own judgment, Ezra gave the order to have the cattle removed to the south pasture.

Her first step was to buy herself a horse and bring down her mother's old saddle. Knowing the value of saving herself for her work, she did not propose to take long tramps over the farm, when a moment's trouble could enable her to ride in one-half the time; and soon, among the hands the sight of her gray pony surmounted by herself, and her broad sun-hat, was not only looked for but welcomed. She always had a kind word for them, and though she insisted on having things done her own way, but her insistance was such that they could but obey, while they marveled at the pleasant manner which hid so much firmness.

In one of her first rides, an empty bottle was filled at the offending brook, and was then dispatched to her old professor in chemistry who confirmed her conjectures. Meanwhile the cattle were improving, but not as quickly as she could have wished. The stables were next examined, and here she found the main difficulty. The drainage, in the light of the science of to-day, was something atrocious. When she contemplated all that was before her she was almost heartsick, but she knew that having put her hand to the plough she must not look back. She recognized, too, the fact that those who have made such things a study are the ones to oversee such work. So she despatched [*sic*] the following note to a fellow graduate:

"You have studied drainage and want practice. Come and drain my farm. I only wonder we are not all dead. When will you come? Telegraph."

Three days later saw Ellen Simpson on the spot and installed as "drainer in chief." And the men? Of course they didn't like being "bossed by a woman," but then there were others found who didn't know quite so much and were consequently twice as valuable. There is nothing which so adds to the value of a servant as being able to receive instruction, and to acknowledge that there are some few things, even in his own line, which are open to discussion as to ways and means. The drainage off her hands, Rebekah set people at work on her fences, and then turned her attention to the house.

"Where can I get a good girl for the kitchen, mother?"

Her mother looked frightened.

"Ye're father won't hear to a girl."

"In the first place he's *not* my father, and in the second, he has nothing to do with it. I thought it was distinctly understood that *I* was running the place. Where can I get a girl?"

"Well, mebbe Almira Giddings would come," answered her mother meekly, secretly rejoiced at having the drudgery taken off her hands in this masterful manner.

"And, mother dear, after the girl comes, won't you take to fixing up the yard a bit? It looks so untidy. I know you haven't had time. I'm not blaming you, but you'll have more time then, and though it is almost too late to plant any vines, I'd like to see those that are out there trimmed and tied up."

She knew in her heart that it would be like breath of a new life to her mother to get out once more among the flowers and plants that she loved, and the look of perfect happiness upon her face, as she pruned here, snipped there, or tied up in another place, was good to see and went far towards reconciling the daughter to the sacrifices she was making.

Matters in the house were put on a new footing. Two coal-oil stoves took the place of the enormous ten-plate concern that had roasted the family all summer long, ever since Rebekah could remember. All the improved utensils were bought, even to "the latest thing in churns," and Almira, who had been very doubtful as to Rebekah and her "new-fangled notions," was soon won over when she found her back and time saved.

Meanwhile the farm work went on apace. Rebekah read and consulted personally all the best authority on approved methods. Dire were some of her mistakes when trying to institute some pet plan of her own; but on the whole, in the account of profit and loss, by far the greater amount might be charged up to profit. The cattle not only did not die, but recovered their health entirely. The chickens rejoiced in their fresh, clean quarters, and though they did nothing marvelous, they did as well as chickens ever do and gave a very fair profit for the time and money expended.

"Well," said Rebekah, laughing, one day, as she entered the dining-room where that young lady sat engaged on some piece of dainty femininity, "old Mr. Salomon is out there and he says he wants 'to see that Simpson gal.' I believe you rejoice in that euphonous title."

"Me! What on earth can he want to see me about?" exclaimed Ellen, dropping her work.

"Don't know! Better go see!"

"Well! if that isn't the *richest!*" said Ellen a few moments later. "What *do* you suppose he wanted?" And she laughed till the tears rolled down her face.

"I can't imagine, I'm sure."

"He wants me to *drain his farm!* And the funniest part of it all is that *he's* the man that aired himself in the cars on the subject of women's education, and 'lowed that women was gettin' so edicated that they didn't know nothin' at all nowadays. Well it certainly is *too* funny for anything but a book."

"It certainly is," answered Rebekah, joining in the merriment.

⚜

"And, of course, she made enough money to pay off the mortgage," I hear some one say. "How lovely!"

Of course she did nothing of the kind. She paid off the mortgage with her own money, but at the end of two years left the farm in her step-father's hands in such a condition, and farmer Kittredge himself with such a stock of new and improved ideas, that he was not only able to keep things running smoothly, but to pay off his indebtedness to Rebekah after a time.

Mrs. Kittredge grew young again, and farmer Kittredge himself did not have nearly so many "miseries" as formerly. He was never again heard complaining of the "hand o' Providence," and Rebekah could go away to her chosen work with a heart full of content. She had proved her theory.

THREE

AN E/MAN/CIPATED WOMAN

WHAT A HEROINE! Competent, confident, and efficacious, within a year's time Rebekah Spofford rescues the family farm, restores her mother's health, and embarks on her "chosen work." Putting "theory into practice," she vanquishes all the obstacles created by misused nature and rampant superstition. Her cultivated understanding guiding her sense of duty, she brings order out of chaos indoors as well as out of doors. Without sacrificing womanly demeanor, she vindicates her teachers, showing neighborhood "doubters" that higher education can render women "more competent" without "spoiling" them. Clearly the author intended Rebekah as a "composite woman,"[1] an appealing embodiment of "modern" female capabilities.

The options open to Rebekah would have been much appreciated by women who read the *Journal* in 1890; female circumstances had changed dramatically during the century. In 1800, women in the United States enjoyed few formal rights. They had little ability to act directly on their own behalf, were viewed as incapable of and inappropriate for independence, and had little space for autonomous action. Although we now know that women of all classes were directly involved in productive labor on farms, in workshops, in crafts, and in salaried and service work,[2] no matter how substantial their economic contributions, they occupied a subordinate status in law, custom, and the prescriptive literature.

Thus, while both contemporaries and historians have provided us with ample illustrations of assertive women, legally, politically, and socially women were seen as "covered by" men; they were effectively the wards of their fathers, husbands, or brothers (or, in the case of enslaved or servant women, their masters).[3] Until the success of campaigns for women's property rights in the 1840s, married women in the United States generally lacked the ability to make contracts on their own, were denied the right to control property (including their own wages), and had no independent legal standing. Even after most states in the Union granted property rights to women, members of the "gentler" sex found it so difficult to put themselves forward in public that none of the organizers of the groundbreaking Woman's Rights Convention of 1848 (including the redoubtable Lucretia Mott and her younger ally Elizabeth Cady Stanton) "felt equal," as one historian delicately put it, to serve as "chairman." In consequence, Mott's husband James came to preside over that much-celebrated event.[4]

Unwelcome in public, women did not even have the power of dominion over their children. Well through the century, custody of minor children (other than infants) was automatically given to fathers in cases of divorce. Women, including those from the best families, had little and limited access to formal education, and their general capacity for learning and intellectual activity was by no means generally accepted. Culturally, behavioral lines were definitively drawn between the sexes, and any deviation might be construed as threatening the very basis of social life.

During the course of the nineteenth century, however, women came to challenge cultural prescriptions that had previously kept them from engagement in political, intellectual, and vocational life and were increasingly successful in entering previously all-male domains. According to many scholars, the meaning of gender was transformed in that period, as women fought for and came to enjoy improved legal and social status and were increasingly free to live autonomously—independent of family control.[5]

Both working-class and middle-class women enjoyed new choices and opportunities not to speak of additional risks in the growing, although often sex-segregated industrial and professional sectors of the economy. Recognition as legal persons, control over property, recourse to divorce, acceptance of women's parental rights through legal custody of children, and various programs of aid for mothers with dependent children widened opportunity structures for married women. Moreover, the expectations imposed by dress, sexual mores, and a retiring demeanor that had limited the activities of prior generations of women diminished along with the dissemination of more flexible and varied costumes, and the acceptance of women who were independent actors in many public arenas.

Increased access to higher education, the emergence of new career opportunities for unmarried educated women, and independent living arrangements facilitated alternative life possibilities and choices. Even in media images, autonomy and independence became more acceptable attributes for women, as indicated by pictures of women riding astride the new even-wheeled bicycle[6] and the increasing numbers of women "typewriters" in the burgeoning office sector.[7] And despite the failure of suffragists to enfranchise women nationally, the efforts to gain political accommodation from the states had been at least partially successful. By 1900, women were enfranchised in many parts of the West and, in states like New York, voted in local school-board elections.

Rebekah is depicted as the beneficiary of these changes. Her hide-bound rural neighbors, apparently ignorant of any number of technological and social innovations, may have doubted that a woman could do anything useful with drains and fields, but Hewitt describes college women as capable of almost any endeavor. And indeed, by 1890, life chances for women had increased considerably. Although women had once been excluded from institutions of higher education, by the end of the century a substantial number of colleges and universities accepted women students, and the graduates of these institutions could look forward to entering some of the professional careers that had formerly been open only to men.

Women not only enjoyed new occupational opportunities, they were increasingly free to live outside the embrace of family control as autonomy and independence became more acceptable female attributes. And that capability represented a major alteration in women's circumstances.

However much the unmarried women that Chambers-Schiller studied may have cherished their mental independence, in the years before the Civil War spinsters were almost never free to live alone. By the turn of the century, in contrast, women who remained unmarried were not only able to support themselves, but were able to establish separate households and develop a social and intellectual life outside of family control. And, as it turned out, they came to be admired precisely because of those freedoms.

Although Edward Bok, who acceded to the *Journal*'s editorship in 1890, was both conventional and conservative in his views, he found much to admire in single professional women, particularly when they remained loyal to the families they left behind. Indeed, as if she were a child of his own making, Rebekah appeared a mere nine months after he took office. But although the *Journal's* editor and his readers might have thought Rebekah attractive and appealing, Hewitt's account of love, duty, and aspiration has hardly proved timeless. Didactic in tone and reading like a recipe, the style now seems wooden, the characters poorly developed, and the humor labored. In the narrative, as in the accompanying illustrations, the heroine's features are so vaguely delineated as to be indistinct. Lacking a compelling plot and deficient in character development, this work would hardly appeal to a modern audience.

Although it may not be worthy of inclusion in anyone's list of "best" stories of the ages, "Rebekah Spofford's Theory" is more than a mere historical curiosity. Given what we have been led to believe about the restrictions women faced a century ago, Rebekah seems to have been remarkably unconstrained. Perhaps even more to the point, the fact that such a character was featured in a periodical dedicated to attracting a mass audience is indicative of her significance as a type.

People experience and express meaning through what sociologist Anne Swidler has called the cultural "toolkit of symbols, stories, rituals, and worldviews."[8] Thus, no story is "universal" and "timeless"; its meaning and impact rest on the assumptions and knowledge of the people who hear or read it. Connections that are immediately obvious in one cultural setting are not available in others, as anthropologist Laura Bohannon learned when she narrated Hamlet's story to an African audience.[9] Tales that are engrossing in some cultures may not enchant others.[10]

So, a story such as Rebekah's, which was considered worth bringing to *Journal* readers in the past but has little appeal now, is likely to indicate the existence of ideas that were taken for granted or understandings that were not seen to require substantiation. Those elements that startle or make little sense to today's reader are historically valuable, however, precisely because those omissions and discontinuities would not have been noticed when the story was published. Thus, Janet Todd argues,

> ideological constructions depend for their effectiveness on their success in tricking themselves out with the appearance of naturalness and disinterestedness, they cannot actually be natural and disinterested without defeating their purpose. However ob-

liquely, and by whatever arts of indirection, ideology is committed to a certain show of presence. The sign of this presence is less the barefaced falsehood, visible for all to see and to challenge, than a kind of tell-tale omission or discursive hiatus. As that which can neither fully declare nor completely disavow itself, ideology is inscribed upon cultural representations in the appropriately subliminal form of microscopic logical rupturings, random discordances, and strategic silences. It is to be found in those aspects of images and discourses that display the lowest degree of intentionality or rational deliberation; those that are therefore offered as the most self-evident and uncontentious.[11]

For this reason, one way to pinpoint shifts in meaning over time is to disinter the hidden mechanisms in a tale, to locate what seem now to be inexplicable silences, logical holes, or apparent contradictions in texts produced in the past. Such methods are particularly useful in exploring ideas about women because, as anthropologist Igor Kopytoff points out, those elements of gender that a culture deems immanent—what is perceived as an inborn and inevitable concomitant of sex—are those that are presented as so self-evident that they need no explanation.[12] So what now appear to be obvious lacunae, or gaps in Hewitt's story, are of interest precisely because they would not have been regarded as problematic by Hewitt and her audience.

Thus, what now seems to have been omitted or discontinuous in this story is as important as what is included or appears to follow logically. Most notably, it is significant that while Hewitt's story was clearly designed to depict the possibilities open to one of the beneficiaries of changing opportunities for women, it described Rebekah's career plans sketchily at best, never troubling to provide an explanation for her heroine's choices. And despite the fact that Rebekah's future lay entirely in her career, Hewitt gave her readers little information about her heroine's intellectual activities or the work she intended to take up. Even more tellingly, this author made no effort to explain what led her protagonist to opt for spinsterhood. In fact, Rebekah's intellectual, vocational, and social aspirations were accorded far less space than the habits and inclinations of her mother and stepfather— the very people she intended to leave behind. Clearly, Hewitt felt no need to explain Rebekah's motives for wanting a career, for going to college, or for remaining single. She must have thought them obvious.

Indeed, Hewitt never really bothered to describe her heroine's aspirations. Rebekah's independence and efficacy was clearly enhanced by three intertwined and defining factors—her education, her vocation, and her unmarried status. But neither she nor her creator apparently felt any need to invoke any warrants or disclaimers to account for the genesis of her life choices or to discuss the circumstances that led Rebekah to college or to teaching as a vocation. The nature of her hopes and the details of her plans for the future were also left to the reader's imagination. Even the nature of the friendship with the skilled Ellen Simpson, who not only had a way with drains but who seems to have been so attached to Rebekah that she gave up whatever plans she may have had and moved in for the year, was curiously unelaborated.

Hewitt must have felt such particulars were unnecessary; the constellation of choices seemed so natural they spoke, as it were, for themselves. This was a life course so generally accepted that the author could dispense with its genealogy. Rebekah must have been such a familiar type that Hewitt didn't even feel the need to introduce her until the tale was almost half told and even then, as in the illustrations that accompanied the story, her features were only vaguely rendered.

In particular, Hewitt's characterization of the benefits of higher education and its link to nascent spinsterhood must have seemed so obvious that neither she nor her editor would have thought to require further elucidation of the connection. Rebekah's unexplored but clear determination to remain unmarried was neither unexpected nor uncommon at the time—college women were viewed as problematic candidates for wedlock. And, in fact, some young women who entered college between 1870 and 1900 conformed to that stereotype—they were more likely to remain unwed than any other group. So strong was this association that one historian has concluded that some substantial proportion of women who went to college in this period sought out higher education because they intended to remain single.[13] That is why, in Hewitt's story, work and family life were depicted as requiring incompatible commitments from women; here as elsewhere the collegiate experience was perceived as drawing women away from marriage and motherhood.[14]

Hewitt bolstered Rebekah's capacity for autonomous action in three ways: she killed off father Spofford, gave her an education that elevated her into a class that was well above that of her progenitors, and conceived of her as less interested in romance than in career. In this way, she simultaneously rendered her protagonist fatherless, economically secure, and authoritative. Sending Rebekah's father to an early grave made it possible for that young woman to have her cake and eat it, too. If Rebekah's father had been alive and had disapproved of higher education for women, a "good" daughter could not have acted without regard to his wishes. Thus, in arranging for Mr. Spofford's demise, Hewitt avoided any hint of filial disobedience. At the same time, by making sure that Rebekah's father provided her with a decent sum (what would have been appositely referred to as an "independence" at the time) in his will, she also eliminated the need for any discussion about the character of Rebekah's sire. Except what might be inferred from the fact that he had money to give and from the deficiencies of his successor, the disposition of his estate foreclosed any possibility that he might demonstrate a proclivity to direct the life of his offspring even after death.

Hewitt's plot assumes that Rebekah could remain free only as long as she remained unmarried and renders her more interested in the former than the latter. If marriage has no place in her plans for the future, no man can command her obedience and nothing in this story even hints at the likelihood that Rebekah has had or desires a heterosexual relationship. Her hopes are tied to her vocation, and her affections lie with other women. As the author felt little need to explain that preference in detail, we might conclude that she assumed homosociality to be an essential element of her protagonist's identity.[15]

Too, the ignorance and foolishness of Rebekah's stepfather, farmer Kittredge, who, as his wife puts it, "might have been much more 'worse,'" amply justifies a rejection of heterosexual relationships. That is why it makes sense that Kittredge should be the most developed character in the story; he creates the little tension and humor that exist in the piece and drives the plot forward. Rebekah's education supports vocational aims (perhaps, it may be inferred, in the field of chemistry, but it is his demeanor that bolsters her choice against wedlock). In this Hewitt, who identified herself as a "Mrs." at least at one point,[16] accepted Susan B. Anthony's "logic of events," which she said, "points to an *epoch of single women*" who choose that estate. So long as "women will not accept marriage *with subjection*, nor men proffer it *without*," Anthony contended, "there, is, there can be, *no alternative*. The woman who will *not be ruled* must live without marriage."[17]

Because there is no source of patriarchal authority in her tale, Rebekah suffers no possibility of conflict between heart and mind, no struggle between duty and inclination. Unfettered by obligations to father, fiancé, or husband and prepared to function only with the support of other women, she can follow her own dictates and yet live up to the highest principles. Removed from the soil, tempered in the fires of academe, and finished by a work of sacrifice, she can devote herself to the needs of her family without giving up her independence. Thus, the motives for her affections need no exploration. She can love and protect her mother even while she is ashamed of her parent's verbal and emotional limitations.

Clearly, erotic preference has no standing in the context of this story—neither the time nor the place was conducive to explicit discussion of such matters. Moreover, as Christina Simmons points out, whatever women did in private, publicly at least, respectable, middle-class women (whether married or single) were thought to be "'passionless' and to be guided more by maternal instinct than sexual desire per se."[18] And that ideology, Nancy Cott argues, which gave women of the "better" sort claims to superior moral qualities, offered unique opportunities for female independence and advancement.[19]

But to the modern reader, sexual preference is not as remote as Hewitt might have wanted it to be. Rebekah is engrossed in a world in which men are only incidental. Her affectional ties have been forged in a homosocial world, and this story not only accepts the normality of such arrangements, it idealizes them. The competencies and confidence this young woman displays are clearly a consequence of her engagement in a single-sex environment, and the author implies that such communities are far more perfect than those that men control.

Moreover, Hewitt takes some pains to indicate that Rebekah is not unique. She suggests, through her cameo of Ellen, that many women of Rebekah's age, whose morals and minds have been improved by higher education and who are not confined by the burdens of marriage, are likely working their own forms of magic in myriad settings. Free from the claims of men, especially men who are their inferiors, and unburdened by the requirements of reproduction, they are here conceived as a force to be reckoned with. Like friend Ellen, they have been instructed in the newest and most effective ways of draining away the muck and restoring the landscape. Ready and able to step in at a moment's notice and educated in the practical applications of scientific practice, how much more might be accomplished if the numbers of such women were to increase?

By the time "Rebekah Spofford's Theory" was published in 1890, the *Ladies' Home Journal* had become the most popular, innovative, and influential, although arguably one of the most conservative, mass-market magazines of the period.[20] Just twenty-four pages in length at the beginning of the year, it was nonetheless preeminent among the numerous publications designed to reach a female audience; it was widely read because women liked it and, conversely, because it was widely read its views were of some consequence to the public. The scholars who have reconstructed its early history have described the *Journal* as instrumental in shaping the vocabulary of gender.[21] Short stories, news, and questions about women's proper roles were commonly and centrally featured in its pages. Helen Damon-Moore, who has written the definitive history of the *Journal's* early development, says it created a forum that continues to this day:

> to foster the popular representation of and discussion of gender issues. In fact, the assumed propensity of women to seek to understand their lives, especially in relation to men, actually informed every feature of the magazine—its general advice articles, short stories, editorial comments and homilies, letters from readers, and even its advertising.[22]

This periodical both responded to and influenced the ideas and practices of several generations of women. Jennifer Scanlon, author of an excellent cultural history of the magazine, notes that it "both modeled and adapted to the expectations of its readers."[23] Catering successfully to the concerns of both audience and producers, the *Journal* can be seen as constituting a kind of cultural exchange point. It consulted and acted on advertisers' needs, staff aims, and readers' wishes and, consequently, its pages reflected, shaped, and reacted to discussions affecting domestic life. Images of unmarried women inscribed in the *Journal's* pages followed what might be construed as the three "r"s of cultural construction—they responded to, replicated, and revised the multiple and sometimes contradictory processes of imagining social categories. In that process, the magazine both helped to shape and confirm a new iconography of spinsterhood.

Despite, or perhaps because of, its focus on marriage and family, the spinster was one of the magazine's stock figures before World War I. Even more important here, although its manifest aim was expanding circulation among women whose main interest lay in improving the domestic realm, the *Journal* carried a fair number of pieces on women who eschewed connubiality. *Journal* authors described spinster life with respect and admiration and portrayed never-marrying women as sophisticated and attractive—although asexual—exemplars of a new form of existence. Thus, Hewitt's approving portrait of Rebekah and her friend not only had ample precedent, it was succeeded by others that were equally complimentary. Often defended and sometimes celebrated, even when occasionally deplored or excoriated, the *Ladies' Home Journal* depicted women who remained single as carving out an alternative life path. Perhaps in consequence, their features revealed both fears and hopes for the future of humanity.

From the *Journal's* earliest days, spinsters were invoked by both married and unmarried contributors of both sexes to define an option for adult women that permitted engagement in rewarding as well as altruistic endeavors and facilitated self-development as well as self-sacrifice. Insofar as a woman refrained from heterosexual commitments she was free to engage herself in the world. Depicted as a member of an elite group, the woman who refrained from marrying shouldered tasks and roles that were deemed inappropriate for her married sisters. At the same time, however, she also garnered rewards that were otherwise unavailable to others of her sex. In this way, *Journal* writers in these years emphasized the extraordinary accomplishments and womanly qualities of unmarried female celibates, recreating them almost as a third sex.

Spinsters made regular appearances in the *Journal* from the very beginning. However, while the treatment of single women was generally positive in the *Journal's* earliest years, under its first editor, Louisa Knapp Curtis, writers mounted few open defenses of spinsterhood as a life choice. Hewitt herself was one of the earliest to explicitly describe spinsterhood as an honorable estate. In 1885, in one of her regular, pseudonymously authored, columns, she objected that the term "old maid" was generally

> in its accepted sense, a term of reproach. Instead of meaning a person it has grown to mean a certain set of faults that are supposed to characterize single women after they have attained their thirtieth year. . . . [M]ost young men seem to imagine that if a woman doesn't marry it is because she has been unfortunate enough to remain unsought . . . [Yet] . . . even if such were the

case, it has been a great blessing to thousands of married men and women that at least one of their sisters has had no opportunity to do the same. The women that have devoted their lives unselfishly to their nieces and nephews and died as quietly as they lived, unhonored and unsung [are legion]. . . . That they never had an opportunity to change their state of single-blessedness, a legion of unwritten romances will give the lie to.[24]

But such a defense was rare. In the early years, under Knapp's editorship, spinsters were generally discussed obliquely rather than directly. They appeared in short stories as caretakers, who could be engrossed by the long-lasting requirements of needy, infirm, aged, or orphaned relatives, or as professional women, with time to devote to the requirements of the job. Story narratives in these years pictured them in the act of succoring others, especially younger relatives.

Although motives for remaining unwed were rarely discussed in this early period, spinsters were neither described as single because they were pitiable nor accorded pity because they were single. A number of authors suggested that women failed to marry less as a result of repugnance for wedlock than because men of the appropriate character were lacking. The anonymous author of an 1885 column, for example, contended that women "would love and marry as readily today as when the earth was new, if they came in contact with men who aroused their respect and admiration." But, she warned, "[t]he order of maidenhood that could content itself with an inferior article of husband merely for the sake of being married, has almost vanished. The young woman of the period has too much character and self-respect to dread being an old maid."[25]

Still, in these pieces, as in Hewitt's column, there was a tension between negative and positive characterizations of women who remained unmarried. Ironically, given later characterizations, early *Journal* contributors depicted spinsters as rather more prone to the sin of narcissism than their married sisters, mainly because they had more leisure and an easier life. For this reason, they were described as more likely to remain physically attractive than their wedded counterparts:

An old maid . . . goes on in a regular routine: breakfast, a walk, feed the poodle and parrot, visit the poor people and give them tracts and marmalade, come home to lunch, embroider four scallops on the last new collar, call on a friend, or receive a call, take dinner, go to an evening meeting if there is one; if not read a letter, or write a letter, put her hair in papers, and retire. . . .

But a married woman! Who can tell what erratic course she may be obliged to pursue during the next twenty-four hours?[26]

Or as Aunt Melissa remarked on seeing her sister-in-law for the first time in some years:

Well sister Jane, you've grown old . . . We old maids keep our youth and good looks, after all, if we don't keep husbands, ha ha![27]

In contrast, the woman who married was far more likely to sacrifice comeliness to domestic exigency:

Who can tell what erratic course she [a married woman] may be obliged to pursue during the next twenty-four hours? First, there is the question whether the other half of her soul will get in at five in the afternoon or twelve at night. Whether she is to dine with him comfortably or sit up uncomfortably. Whether, if he comes, he will be in a good humor or not. So much depends on whether Jones has paid that bill or whether things look straight about politics. . . .
    Men are like fleas—now you have 'em, now you haven't. Married and settled! With babies who have colic at midnight, and croup about five o'clock in the morning; with children who may have measles, scarlet-fever, chicken-pox and mumps at any moment and whose object in life seems to be to fall down stairs or set the house on fire! With a traditional mother-in-law who can't believe her dear son is properly fed or patched, and who lays all the wrongs of her life to "poor Jane who perhaps would do better if she knew how;" with cooks who take offense, and chambermaids who get married and waiter-girls who give warning and break china; with new babies and old nurses and never

a quiet moment from the morning getting up till the time for lying down.[28]

But despite, or maybe because of, her lack of encumbrances, the un-married woman was described as a useful and helpful influence. The *Journal* of this epoch generally promulgated the view that spinsters were valuable assets to the family writ both small and large. Its most fulsome praise was reserved for maiden aunts who became substitute mothers not only for their own nieces and nephews but for other orphaned children as well; they were lovingly treated in both stories and commentary. Like their married sisters, women who remained single were rendered most sympathetically when it could be said that they were, as two historians put it: "feminine in their ways, gentle, good, sweet, demure with men, carrying out their jobs in a nurturing way."[29] And, countering any assumptions that single women were masculin-ized, many of the articles and items published in the magazine emphasized both their benevolence and their womanly graces.

Yet even in this early period, the magazine devoted space to the accomplishments of unmarried women who were unusually successful, such as the

lady shorthand writer in the western part of New York State who earns $8,000 a year [and the] . . . lady in the same business who makes $5,000 a year, and . . . a lady short-hand reporter for the Courts, whose yearly earnings are $9,000 a year.[30]

The special abilities of single women, their initiative, and their financial successes were recorded in many of the short news items that provided filler for the early issues, thus

Miss Leila J. Robinson, a bewitching young lawyer of Boston, went out to settle in Seattle a short time ago. She has been winning cases from the best lawyers of the territory, and the people now talk about making her a judge. This modern Portia is also said to be a good newspaperwoman.[31]

By invoking single women in the context of career success, the *Journal* implicitly acknowledged the link between marital status and occupational possibilities. Such pieces portrayed the life of such women as both attractive and rewarding. Spinsters were depicted as most successful, however, when they supported domesticity even as they avoided reproduction. Thus, while a front-page story about the only woman lighthouse keeper in the United States described her heroism (she saved four boys from drowning when she was sixteen years old), it devoted at least as much attention to the domestic improvements she had been able to effect in that usually masculine domain. The piece lovingly detailed the "clean and white" kitchen that "betokens the exceptional housewife," the sitting room furnished with "books and flowers and sunshine," the white lace curtains that graced her parlor and the "sleeping" room, that "like herself . . . is bright, hung with pictures everywhere, and full of the belongings of a womanly woman."[32]

Of course, it is also true that some of the spinsters who inhabited the magazine's pages between 1884 and 1890 while Knapp was editor were unsympathetic figures. A number were depicted as helpless, indolent, overly devoted to appearances, cold, or authoritarian or controlling. But such characteristics were deemed equally unattractive in married women. In general, writers for the early *Journal* were highly critical of anything that might be defined as self-centered or narcissistic behavior on the part of any member of the "fair" sex. Admirable females, whether married or unmarried, sacrificed and devoted themselves to those around them, but most especially to children.

Women who were self-absorbed failed in this regard and, thus, were treated as deserving of scorn, contempt, or pity, whatever their marital status. So, for example, in "Poor Mrs. Taylor," a story published in 1884, a complaining, unhappy, and controlling mother who tries to keep her children from a normal social life loses the affections of her daughters and, worse yet, sees two of her sons go bad.

In short, the magazine's first editor supported the view of one of her authors that not "every woman was intended for a wife," and that "[m]any serve God and humanity nobly by remaining single."[33] And single women were deemed most fulfilled and worthy of respect when their devotion to career did not impede their willingness to make sacrifices for family or become surrogate mothers to orphaned children. So, even as the magazine emphasized "feminine" and "domestic" virtues, it celebrated women who chose nonmarital alternatives, and emphasized their capacity to support themselves by their own efforts and to make homes for themselves, attributes not seen as characteristic in previous generations even if, as Chambers-Schiller shows, defense of that "blessed" estate had been current in the United States long before the Civil War.[34]

Knapp's successor in 1890, Edward Bok, devoted far more space to women who had decided against marriage than did his predecessor, and his attention, especially in the first decade of his reign, was laudatory. His *Journal* promulgated the view that spinsterhood was a voluntary condition and, under his leadership, the magazine paid increased attention to women who did not marry. On the editorial page, Bok waxed poetic over their accomplishments, making frequent references to their contributions to the human family writ large, as well as to their kin. In his July 1890 editorial, for example, he lauded the

> hundreds of women to-day who have never married because of some special mission in life, either in their own families, or to the world-at-large, which they felt they could better accomplish if untrammeled by domestic cares. By their self-sacrifice, these women are heroines.

While "[y]ou and I may believe that it is for the greatest happiness of all women that they should marry" he said, "that is no reason why we should not respect those who by their lives show that they have decided otherwise." He went on to defend this order of womanhood in terms that permeated much of the imagery of spinsters published throughout the period:

> There are countless families to-day who will lose their brightest and most comforting members when the breath of her who never uttered the marriage vow returns to its Maker. Angels of comfort are those 'old maids' of American homes, every day of their lives teaching us anew some noble trait of self-sacrificing and ever glorious womanhood.

Bok described single women who found ways to better the world for others as "Uncrowned Heroines." Like nuns, they

> never married because of some special mission in life, either in their own families, or to the world-at-large, which they felt they could better accomplish if untrammeled by domestic cares.[35]

Thus, Hewitt's story fit well into Bok's scheme of things. He made college women like Rebekah *Journal* "girls." In 1890, as he took over the editor's chair, the magazine offered the "girl of 16 years of age, or over" who sold the most full-price subscriptions in 1890 "a complete education at Vassar College . . . or any other American college." That was, indeed, a handsome prize. It was described as including "all expenses of tuition, board, &c" "in every branch of study . . . irrespective of the time involved." Friends, fun, hard work, and religious training, the announcement stated, awaited the lucky winner. The value of the prize was highlighted in a July 1890 article celebrating life at Vassar College, which emphasized the normalcy of its students, the glories of the campus, and the beneficial effects of its programs.[36]

Bok has never been described as other than conservative;[37] he was, for example, opposed to political rights for women. Yet these views did not lead him, as it did others of his generation, to excoriate female collegians nor directly to attack career women. Rather, from his very first days in the editor's chair, the *Journal* both celebrated and normalized the college and career experience even as other prominent figures, presumably less enlightened, did not.[38] It is possible that by the early 1890s Bok saw commercial possibilities in coverage designed to appeal to women who hoped to enter institutions of higher education. But given the relative infrequency of college-educated women in the population and the magazine's targeted audience, it seems unlikely.[39] It is, therefore, rather more likely that he considered such women at least as appealing to his desired audience as worth appealing to.

Rebekah, for example, is admirable not only because of her exposure to academic subject matter but because of the moral improvement engendered by exposure to the world of higher learning. Removal from the simple and rustic scenery of her birth to the advantages of collegiate life, her diction no less than her enhanced skills came to define her, but also to separate her from her origins. Yet she lost neither conscience nor moral center through the experience. Instead, her sensibilities and affections could be represented as purified and strengthened in the educational forge. Diverging from her mother's path in vocation, as well as in grammar, she was still willing to engage in the most humble and menial of household tasks, and to consider the wants of family before her own.

But Bok did more than praise the woman who never married for her selflessness. This new, although not always constant, friend also gave her numerous opportunities to define and defend herself. During his regime, maiden ladies were not only accorded room in features, commentary, and stories, they were also given space to present themselves as the heroines of their own lives. Single women writers found a bully pulpit in the magazine's pages; they were given and took the opportunity to describe, defend, and elevate their condition. Indeed, Hewitt may not have needed to justify Rebekah's choices because these authors took such pains in explaining theirs. From 1890 to World War I, in each of the years I surveyed, the magazine published at least one autobiographical piece, with bylines that indicated authorship by unmarried women. The frequency with which these features appeared indicate that they found an interested, if not sympathetic, audience in the magazine's readers, as well as, presumably, in the editor who printed them.

Such pieces were not unique to the *Ladies' Home Journal*. They belong to a genre that is sometimes referred to as "apologia" (a confession containing a warrant or justification for one's life). As Ruth Freeman and Patricia Klaus document, self-accounts written by women who identified themselves as spinsters appeared in a variety of what might be called the "better" periodicals of the period, and they were all strikingly similar. They followed a standard format and contained a set of common elements. Uniformly, for example, these accounts ended by asserting the meritorious attributes of women who remain unwed, their usefulness to their families of origin, their worldly accomplishments, and their superiority to the common run of women. This intertextuality reflects the existence of a stock cultural plot, one that might be labeled "the spinster's canon." That very consistency suggests a larger rhetorical purpose.[40]

Thus, while they were offered as the histories and confessions of particular individuals, their tone was polemical. And although they were written in the autobiographical style, their authors were identified only by pseudonyms—"An Old Maid," "Phyllis Perchance," "A Spinster Who Learned to Say No." These pieces were salvos fired in the context of a long-running debate about women's capacities and desires. They set about defining an insurgent group—those who took an alternate path. Functioning as what one theorist of social movements describes as a "mobilizing narrative," they deployed oppositional meanings within a conventional form,"[41] legitimating insurgency in the comfort of "familiar stories." In them, the ideology that structured "accepted hierarchies" was undermined by the innovative reconstitution of standard plot elements.[42]

Reverberating and echoing themes developed elsewhere in the pages of the *Journal*, the spinster confessions justified rejection of normative standards of behavior and offered an intriguing view of "womanly" alternatives. Emphasizing their own feminine qualities—delicacy, domesticity, and willingness to sacrifice self to others—these representatives of the alternate path countered those who dared to depict them as masculinized. More, they implied, spinsterhood was inevitable for the best of their sex. Describing themselves as driven by the requirements of emotional sensibility, intellectual superiority, and managerial capacity, they argued that remaining single was as much a vocation as a fate. For that reason, these pieces inevitably devoted as much attention to describing their chances to wed as the joys of their estate.

In this vein, each of the pieces I saw included a disclaimer indicating that the author had been offered at least one (and usually more than one) opportunity to marry, but had rejected it. Thus, the "Old Maid" (the first of the apologists), who described herself as a woman of "forty, healthy, said to be good-looking, well-educated and always well-dressed," protested that "[L]ike most women who are pleasant to look upon, cheerful in . . . manner, and neat in . . . mode of dressing," she had been offered several chances to marry. She had remained single out of choice rather than necessity, she insisted. And she observed condescendingly, "My friends, every woman in this world who wants to, can marry."[43]

The "Old Maid" had rejected her suitors because of their faults of character. The first, a man she "came very near loving . . . enough," was "bright, handsome" and magnetic, but he was a "hard" drinker and she feared for the consequences. But she rejected two other, quite eminent prospects, as well: a respectable clergyman, because he was so domineering that her life with him could only have been filled with "discordance and wretchedness," and a man who was very well known, who required a wife who was ready to devote herself to him and all his interests. "I never married" she said, "because I never met a man whose love covered the faults in his character which I was sure would make me unhappy."[44] In 1890, a woman who named herself "Phyllis Perchance" also wrote that she was unlikely to marry, having turned down five men already. Cited by Bok as one of the most successful items ever published in the magazine, her article concluded, "The man is yet to come who can strike a spark from [my] heart."[45]

Twenty years later, "A Spinster Who Had Learned to Say No" employed the same formula to describe her own rejection of three suitors.[46] Bowing to the notion that marriage was the primary aim of every woman, she wrote, "I should have preferred to say yes." However, her tart continuation indicated the opposite.

> I make no attempt to prove that the grapes are sour; I frankly admit that they hang too high. I do not belong to the ranks of wage earning spinsterhood because I prefer selfish ease to the responsibilities of wedlock, nor yet because I am in mad pursuit of a career; I am there because no man whom I could accept has ever asked me to marry him.[47]

Obviously, for the "Spinster Who has Learned to Say No," there were many reasons to remain unmarried: avoidance of the "responsibilities" of married life, enjoying the pleasures attendant on a "career," and, most important for her, recognizing the deficiencies of her suitors.

Like the apologists who preceded her, she claimed to have had several offers of marriage, the first from an old family friend, the second from a man who was "excellent match in the eyes of the world," and whom she loved "in the popular sense of the word," and finally by a "widower whom men honored." She turned down the first because although she found him "congenial," did not want to do the wrong of accepting "the sacred trust of wifehood without love." She gave up the next, even though she was "happy in his presence and thrilled to his touch." He was, she said, too "supremely self-centered," and his sneering response to her refusal made her glad of her choice. The last was, she said, the most tempting because it offered the most financial security. But, she said "our tastes were widely separated," and she did not feel able to marry without "the pure gold of real companionship."

The *Journal's* staff seems to have concurred with these pseudonymous spinsters in evaluating men negatively both in Knapp's and Bok's time. Leafing through the issues published during the magazine's first quarter century, I came to appreciate the fact that even as the magazine lauded wedded life in the abstract, contributors had enough serious misgivings to be wary of the idea of marriage for its own sake, and they were not reluctant to share their reservations with their readers.

Perhaps the possibilities for remaining single gave criticisms of contemporary manhood an extra wallop. In any event, the magazine seemed as intent on warning young women about the problems and difficulties that might follow wedlock as on romanticizing it. Some contributors had apparently seen sufficient numbers of bad marriages to temper their enthusiasm for the institution. Like the woman who turned down a "bright and hand-some" but hard-drinking suitor, they may have had intimate acquaintance with one of the "the wretched wives, the miserable children and the un-happy homes that had resulted from such [badly advised] marriages."[48] Others, like the unnamed author of an 1885 piece, saw a decline in the quality of men as a serious problem. Citing an informant who thought that "the inefficient class of men" were increasing at "alarming" rates, she (or he, as the author of this piece had no byline) described "the material in the way of husbands" to be both "unattractive" and "unreliable."[49]

References to problematic marriages (frequently although sometimes indirectly attributed to male deficiency) were almost inevitably linked to an analysis of the "other" option—staying single. As one author advised young women: "Your great fear needn't be whether you can 'get married' or not, but whether you may not be tempted to marry too soon, or unworthily."[50] In such a manner, "A Spinster Who Has Learned to Say No" reflected on her life after she had refused three proposals of marriage and the security that would have followed:

> I have seen many women in the almshouse who wore wedding rings. My earning powers are no more liable to wane than are those of a man. I surely know far more of finance than does a woman whose husband has neglected to provide a safeguard for old age. But—if it comes to that—I shall have lived, and I can endure the years with my memories.

Whatever might have been lacking in a spinster's life, the *Journal* did not seem to regard the absence of sexual activity as significant. Far from it. Given the magazine's content or lack of it, erotic joys were apparently reckoned of far less value than the domestic situation that accompanied wedlock. Thus, while a spinster's chastity may well have been presumed, it never required mention either as deprivation or benefit. On the contrary, if the purveyors of *Journal* saw any institution as central to the fulfillment of women's desires, it was not marriage but motherhood.

As opposed to romantic love, which journal contributors often treated with wary concern, and sometimes described as a snare and a delusion, maternality was uniformly depicted as the ultimate in womanly fulfillment. The home with children was portrayed as the most rewarding of domiciles and described as the basic feminine objective. In contrast, unmarried women were described as deprived only when they had no relation to children. Thus, although the "Spinster Who Has Learned to Say No" did not regret the loss of her suitors or her lack of a husband, she did bemoan her childless state:

> At times a pain clutches at my heart when I enter the swinging doors of a real home. I see a mother bending over her babes; a wife in the strong circle of her husband's arm. That night my pillow may be wet with tears. But I recall some white-faced, dull-eyed woman who has accepted dross for the gold of a true mating and I am glad that I learned to say "No."[51]

Substitutes for motherhood were readily available, however. Thus, the "Old Maid" of 1890 not only found solace in caring for her parents and her small nieces and nephews, but experienced love and joy though taking in the orphaned children of her first (alcoholic) suitor. The "Spinster Who Has Learned to Say No" also counted herself fulfilled through her relation to the young:

> I am contented with my lot. . . . Little children nestle in my arms. The title of "Auntie" is very sweet as it falls from the lips of a prattling babe. Youths and maidens sit at my feet and clasp my hand in their strong young fingers.

These pieces reinforce scholarly contentions that while career opportunities for women mushroomed in the period between the Civil War and World War I, they were generally restricted to women who were willing to forgo marriage. This conjunction of circumstances not only produced a political opportunity for advocates of women's advancement, it also catapulted the spinster into new prominence. A more powerful heroine—one like Rebekah Spofford—superseded the retiring, family-oriented, sometimes childish spinster of some of the *Journal*'s earlier fiction who was, at best, fitted for an auxiliary role. And the benefits of her situation were so obvious that they required no explanation.

However, the impact of generalized figures is never straightforward, and while some of the implications of the magazine's treatment of spinsterhood may be extracted through textual analysis, the ultimate effect of those portrayals is far more difficult to determine. The number of autobiographical justification's of spinsterhood that appeared in the *Journal* clearly indicate the existence of negative views of that estate. Certainly unmarried women figured large in the minds of those who were concerned about the state of the family as well as those who rejoiced in women's new accomplishments. At the very least, spinster iconography was contested territory and while advocates of female advancement embraced the accomplishments of women who devoted themselves to the human family at large, and traditionalists warned of dire consequences if women were encouraged to abandon the domestic realm, consumers brought their own interpretations to the pictures painted in the magazine. Thus, invocations of college maidens like Rebekah were far more than mere reactions to the behavior of a small group of women; they frequently served as the basis for claims about what was and what was not appropriately "womanly." Whatever readings this imagery permitted, however, emphasis on the affinity of women (as a group) for domestic life, not to speak of the difficulty they were likely to encounter in opting for the "alternate path," allowed for a negative as well as positive translation of the single estate.

FOUR

"SHE HAS DELIBERATELY SHUT THE DOOR OF OPPORTUNITY"

MARGARITA SPALDING GERRY aimed at advancing the cause of domesticity in the second of the college-girl stories, "The Woman Who Threw Herself Away."[1] To that end, she had her heroines decide to give up their professional aspirations in order to embrace the joys of motherhood. Gerry herself had begun a career as a freelance writer after her husband's death in 1908.[2] Perhaps she was reacting to the pleasures and exigencies of her own experience or she may just have wanted to deliver what she thought the *Journal* would buy. Whatever the reason, the moral she wanted to impart was undermined by the content of her story. In counterposing the lifestyles of single career women with their married sisters, she emphasized the glamour of the former and the costs of the latter, portraying spinsterhood as far more rewarding than married life—at least for college women.

THE WOMAN WHO THREW HERSELF AWAY
by Margarita Spalding Gerry, 1913

If you had been deposited in the Main Building on the way from the planet Mars you would still have known it was holidaytime. The girl—were she

She Woman Who Threw Herself Away

By Margarita Spalding Gerry
Author of Heart and Chart, etc.
Illustrations by Arthur E. Becher

IF YOU had been deposited in the Main Building on the way from the planet Mars you would still have known it was holidaytime. The girl—were she Freshman or Senior—whom you met in the hall had forgotten to endow herself with the lines of careworn responsibility that she wouldn't have been seen without during termtime. Moreover you tripped over trunk-straps. And a fluffy-haired maiden who bent over her trunk-tray had the unmistakable gleam of frivolous anticipation in her eyes as she delicately inflated with tissue paper the rudimentary sleeves of her gauzy dancing frocks. But this gleam was absent from the eyes of a young woman who came quickly down the hall and knocked at the door of Number 141. She was a dark, handsome girl, who bore herself as buoyantly as a properly gowned, properly groomed, hygienically exercised modern Senior in one of the largest colleges for women should do. The girl who was packing her trunk looked up with a flicker of mischief in the smile she nodded at the Senior. Number 141 belonged to a popular young "Faculty," and that relation which Helen Standish cherished with reverence as an uplifting friendship passed in college-girl parlance as a "crush."

"Oh, Miss Metcalf," Helen said eagerly as she closed the door behind her, "I have word of poor Emma."

A woman rose from before a desk that was strewn with papers and notebooks. The soft, fair hair curled babyishly around her temples. One wavy lock even strayed in front of her eyeglasses, impeding for a moment the glance of a pair of very keen blue eyes. But it was the mouth that arrested attention. Rather small than large, and softly red and tenderly sweet, it gave the lie direct to the austere brow and the eyeglasses, and it was, though conscious dignity with which she moved. "Is Emma in trouble? But of course she would be. Why *would* she do it? To give up the chance I got her of being housekeeper at Hendley, and throw herself away

"A Deep Voice Sounded, Followed by Peals of Laughter. Still Miss Metcalf Was Shut Up With the Little Ones"

Freshman or Senior—whom you met in the hall had forgotten to endow herself with the lines of careworn responsibility that she wouldn't have been seen without during termtime. Moreover you tripped over trunk-straps. And a fluffy-haired maiden who bent over her trunk-tray had the unmistakable gleam of frivolous anticipation in her eyes as she delicately inflated with tissue paper the rudimentary sleeves of her gauzy dancing frocks. But this gleam was absent from the eyes of a young woman who came quickly down the hall and knocked at the door of Number 141. She was a dark, handsome girl, who bore herself as buoyantly as a properly gowned, or properly groomed, hygienically exercised modern Senior in one of the largest colleges for women should do. The girl who was packing her trunk looked up with a flicker of mischief in the smile she nodded at the senior. Number 141 belonged to a popular young "Faculty," and that relation which Helen Standish cherished with reverence as an uplifting friendship passed in college-girl parlance as a "crush."

"Oh, Miss Metcalf," Helen said eagerly as she closed the door behind her, "I have word of poor Emma."

A woman rose from before a desk that was strewn with papers and notebooks. The soft, fair hair curled babyishly around her temples. One wavy lock even strayed in front of her eyeglasses, impeding for a moment the glance of a pair of very keen blue eyes. But it was the mouth that arrested attention. Rather small than large, and softly red and tenderly sweet, it gave the lie direct to the austere brow and the eyeglasses, and the cool, conscious dignity with which she moved. "Is Emma in trouble? But of course she would be. Why *would* she do it? To give up the chance I got her of being housekeeper at Hendley, and throw herself away on that man! And at her age too!"

In her indignation Miss Metcalf threw herself down on the draped and cushion-heaped couch. She put out her hand and drew her adorer down beside her. That was because she knew the girl expected it. With an expression of acute sentiment Helen possessed herself of the young "Faculty's" hand. Miss Metcalf stirred restlessly. As soon as she knew a girl was fond of her the undue fervor and abjectness of her devotion always palled and was obscurely embarrassing. Helen she was genuinely fond of and she had thought it was going to be different with her.

"What reasons did Emma give, Miss Met—Charlotte?" asked the devotee timidly. Although she had been given permission to use the name of the elder woman when they were alone she always felt presumptuous when she did so.

Under pretext of putting back a straying lock of hair Miss Metcalf got her embarrassed hand away. " 'Reasons'?" she responded with a shade of irritability. "If she had any reasons she wouldn't have done it. When I asked her what a woman of her age could possibly find desirable in marrying a middle-aged German butcher without a penny to his name and with an indecently large family, a man who would expect her to slave as she had never done before—clean, cook, wash and iron, sew and mend for him and his eight children—she couldn't find a word to say."

Helen opened her mouth impulsively, then flushed rosy-red and shut it again. After all how could there possibly be any association between the emotions of a middle-aged, hard-featured charwoman and her own soft tumult of feeling over things that Jack said? It seemed impossible to speak of anything that might be considered sentimental before the fastidious isolation, the delicate, aloof maidenliness that she could feel in Miss Metcalf. It was she who had urged Helen to try herself in the advanced study of chemistry before she admitted any complication as disturbing as a lover into her life. That was one reason why she was not to go home this holiday

time. Jack might be even now opening her letter—hurt—mystified——.
She winked hard before she hastened to agree with her oracle:

"Yes, I am sure it was very foolish of Emma," she said faintly. "After
all, Emma did have a very good mind. It always seemed so dreadful to think
of her rubbing up floors and scrubbing windows for the girls when her
ambition had been to teach school."

"And now she has deliberately shut the door of opportunity in her
own face," said the young instructor, with compressed lips. "To tell the truth
I'm so indignant with her for being such an idiot that it's hard to be fully
sympathetic. But I suppose it's a plain case of duty to hunt her up. We ought
to see what we can do for her."

"When can we go?" asked Helen dutifully.

"Perhaps we would better try to get there Tuesday," said Miss Metcalf
resignedly. Helen winced. Tuesday was Christmas Eve; and that did seem
such a forlorn thing to do. "I'd like to get it off my mind before Christmas,"
went on the young instructor. "We'll go early enough to get back here and
dress and still get to the theater in good time. You can't afford to miss a word
of a Shaw play. And I'd hate to have one minute spoiled of this perfect time.
I am afraid you have sacrificed a good deal to have it with me."

There was real warmth of affection in the kiss which the clear-eyed
young instructor brushed across the girl's cheek. It almost consoled Helen
for the hurt wonder in her mother's letter and for the affecting picture she
could conjure up without even closing her eyes, of Jack reading hers.

Emma's home—they found it too amusing to think of her as Mrs. Schnorren;
Emma was so distinctly a spinster—was, as they had expected, in a poor
quarter of the city. And the wreaths of green at the two little windows were
pathetically meager.

"Poor Emma! I almost dread to see her," said the younger girl pity-
ingly. "Even when we knew her she never used to have an ounce of flesh
on her. And now I supposed she is fairly ghastly."

But the door was opened so suddenly in response to their knock that
the sigh of sympathy never got beyond Helen's lips. A woman stood in the
doorway. She was a broad, rosy person. The crisp, blue-and-white-checked
gingham of her dress was stretched tautly over her substantial proportions,
and she beamed upon the two who stood before her.

"Does Mrs. Schnorren live here?" asked Miss Metcalf, unrecognizing.

But Helen was staring at the apparition in wonder.

"Don't you recognize me, Miss Metcalf?" said the broad and rosy Emma Schnorren, beaming still more warmly on them. "Well, I *have* gained a little since I saw you." She smoothed down her apron complacently. "My husband says he likes me best this way."

"Oh—how stupid of me! But you've changed so! We have just found out where you live, Emma," said Miss Metcalf, to cover their confusion. "And we wanted to see how you were getting along."

There she stopped. All of the remarks she had in her mind were based upon a commiseration for Emma's sad lot; and that line of conversation did not seem to apply. So she found herself tongue-tied.

Mrs. Schnorren was more than equal to the occasion. She pounced upon her visitors and drew them into the cabbage scented entry. "Here I am forgetting my manners!" she said. "Letting you stand outside in the cold. I was that surprised to see you it drove everything else out of my mind. But I'm right down glad. Come right in"—she hesitated and looked elaborately around the little entry to be sure there was no eavesdropper—"and I'll show you the children's Christmas presents—that is, if I can get rid of the little tikes for a minute. Tony and Clarchen are beginning to suspect something and are just eternally snooping around."

The two visitors found themselves in a bright little dining-room. There were flourishing plants in the sunniest window, and a tall, pink-checked girl with two heavy blond braids down her back was singing joyously as she removed the dishes after what had evidently been a hearty midday dinner.

"That's right, Greta," said the stepmother heartily. "This is our eldest girl, Greta," she explained parenthetically. And the flushed maiden bobbed a funny little curtsy. "Now if you'll just put the cover on the table and do the dishes for me maybe we'll be able to get ahead with the tree. Do you think we've given them enough to fill them up?" she asked her stepdaughter anxiously.

Greta, unable to speak as yet before these august guests, nodded her assurance.

"My, but I'm glad you were home from school today Grety; you certainly are a comfort!" said Emma as the girl whisked on a gay table-cover and carried her trayful of soiled dishes out of the room.

Emma sat down opposite her guests with a surprisingly comfortable visiting look upon her face—Emma, who in the past had bestowed upon all conversation that did not regard her work only an anxious and grudging attention. But now they found no opportunity to put to her the question regarding her welfare which they had come to ask. Instead, they found themselves answering questions themselves: "Is that pretty Miss Ames in your class going to marry the young man whose photographs she has all over her room?" or, "Hasn't that youngest Ayres girl any beau yet? I always thought she was too pretty a girl to teach school."

Miss Metcalf had a rising flush upon her face.

Finally Mrs. Schnorren started. "But what have I been thinking of not to have shown you the baby and the twins?" in a tone of acute self-reproach.

Evidently not to pass around enjoyment of these little ones was, to the house of Schnorren, neglect of the most outrageous kind. Dutifully the college women followed up the steep and narrow stairs.

On a big bed in the front room slept two pretty pink and white, blond children, a little boy and a little girl, the warm chubby arm of the girl around the boy's creased neck. Stopping by them only long enough to pull the comfort up around their shoulders Emma beckoned her guests rapturously to the cribside. And there all three held their breaths.

With half the cover masterfully pushed back, one fat dimpled leg thrust straight out from under it, pink, cushiony fists flung back against the pillow, lay the baby. There never could have been a baby more adorable. And although his baby's funny name was Schnorren; although the crib had wooden slats, and no external grace enshrined him save perfect cleanliness; although it was highly possible that a lifetime of lowly toil stretched out before him; and although the softly rounded temples might cover only mediocre brains, the abounding health and robust beauty with which he was endowed breathed from him in touching majesty. And the three women stood and worshiped at his shrine. His breath was softly taken and loitered out in sweetness. As they hung over him the pink, moist lips trembled into little wistful bud.

With a soft, yearning murmur Emma Schnorren bent over and fondled his forehead cautiously. The touch of her lips was as gentle as love could make it, but the caress vaguely disturbed his dreams. His downy brows knit and he stretched his little fists out and yawned prodigiously.

"Ain't he the darling?" Emma whispered. A soft touch had passed over her harsh features, leaving a tremulous sweetness of eyes and lips that makes any woman lovely. Then she straightened herself up: "It makes me that mad to think of his poor mother having all the pains of him and having to leave all the sweetness of him to another woman's arms!" There were tears in her eyes now.

Neither of these satiric young women saw anything humorous in this passion of sympathy for her husband's dead wife. For the moment an older and more mysterious loyalty held them than even that of woman for man.

It was only an instant, however, that peaceful sentiment reigned. The next instant Greta came into the room. The distress that was written on her broad, low forehead had unloosed her tongue.

"I'm afraid we'll never get the tree trimmed in time," she said tragically. "Father has just sent word by the boy who brought our sausages that he cannot be spared, and Hans has many trips yet to make with the delivery wagon. And Ludwig and I alone cannot finish it in time and yet fill the plates for the children. *Die Kuchen* have not had the strings put through them, and that takes such a long time. And the gifts have come from Tantling and from Onkel Hermann. And Tony and Clärchen are something awful!"

"I'll come, Greta," Mrs. Schnorren said good-humoredly. "I'm forgetting everything today. I suppose it is because I didn't get to bed until this morning." She yawned generously as she put the baby's dimpled leg back under the cover. Greta had bustled self-importantly away.

This was the opening that made Miss Metcalf's postponed inquiries possible. "Don't you have to work dreadfully hard, Emma?" she asked solicitously.

"Not anything like as hard as I used to do." Emma's voice implied that she was on the defensive. "My husband won't let me do a thing outside the house."

" 'Outside the house,' I should think not!" The young instructor was instantly indignant. "You must have too much for your strength to do here."

"Oh, I don't know; the house is very convenient. And the older children help," Emma said weakly.

"Don't you do all the cooking?"

"Greta fixes the vegetables for me when she gets home from school in time. She's as smart a child as I ever saw——"

"And the washing?"

"Of course I do that. But it's only for the family."

"And the ironing?"

"I'd like to see myself letting any one else do my ironing!" The catechized one mustered up some spirit.

"Nobody could iron or clean in my own house to suit me."

"Who does the sewing and the mending?"

"The Unexpected Guests Roused Themselves to Remember That All This Had Not Been in Their Program"

"Greta does the darning. And you have no idea how smart Clarchen is in picking out the bastings. Then I can sew in the evenings."

"What time do you get to bed, Emma?"

"Well, now really, Miss Metcalf, nobody has any call to ask me that. But I suppose it's because you used to know me before I got married. Well, it isn't often that I don't get to bed by twelve. And I sleep grand except when the baby has the croup or the twins get uncovered——"

"I remember when she used to say she wasn't good for anything if she lost her sleep," Helen murmured in an aside to Miss Metcalf.

But Emma went on: "And I don't have to get up any morning but Monday before five o'clock. And my husband always——"

" 'Five o'clock!' " Miss Metcalf repeated with horror. "Your husband ought to be ashamed to make you work so hard."

"I don't work any harder than I want to. And you can see for yourself that it doesn't hurt none!" Emma Schnorren spoke with spirit. "And I don't work any harder than he does. Why he never lets me get out of bed until he has the kitchen fire made and both the base-burners started. And Sunday, when he might lie abed like some men I know of, he's up helping me with the children. He takes all the middle ones out for a walk in the country so I can have my Sunday afternoons as quiet as you please, with Greta here to wheel out the baby. Nobody has it any easier than I have. And we're doing fine. Why we've almost paid for this house. I never thought to own my own house."

The color had risen in her face and her eyes sparkled. Evidently this was not the moment for probing. Exchanging glances of pity for Emma's fatuously blinded eyes, for the time being they gave up their quest.

As they descended they saw the flushed Greta holding the door of the parlor against the determined onslaughts of Tony and Clarchen. Nothing but the slight distinction between short, well-filled-out trousers and short, equally well-filled-out petticoats differentiated obstreperous Tony from boisterous Clarchen. Both were short-haired; both red-faced and patently well-nourished; both had round eyes of expressionless pale blue. Emma scattered the rebellious ones with an assumption of severity which was belied by the indulgent wink with which she accompanied her aside to the guests: "Tony's jealous because Ludwig is to be allowed to help trim the tree. And Clarchen always follows Tony. But I *must* keep them from seeing the tree before it's ready."

The two saw fit to scurry away with a great show of haste. And when Mrs. Schnorren and Greta entered the elect chamber it seemed, somehow, to be the natural thing for the guests to follow. The parlor was a square little box of a room. Its bright prosperity was today only the background for a cheerful riot of green and red Christmas decoration. Red and green paper garlands were strung along the ceiling and men, crisscross, over the gilt chandelier; and all the incredibly unlovely Teutonic and Yankee ancestors were wreathed in loyal greenery or crowned with sprays of artificial holly with stiff, cloth leaves and red-glass berries.

In a corner not far from the clear red glow of the base-burner a sturdy little spruce tree had been erected. A tall, slender boy with a dark, romantic face—the odd one, evidently, in this flaxen-haired family—was unwrapping and sorting into piles the Christmas-tree ornaments from the depths of a huge pasteboard box that lay before him on the floor. He was considering them all—balls, chains, tinsel, stars—with the dreamy look of a painter before the freshly laid colors of his palette.

"Do go get *die Kuchen*, Greta," said Mrs. Schnorren. "They're on a platter in the pantry."

On the way out the girl threw her arms around her stepmother's neck and gave her an impetuous hug. Emma suddenly blushed with a pretty shyness.

"Now we must get to work, Ludwig"—her New England soul made her feel that sentiment was something to be expiated—"it's past four o'clock now, and the only time your father can get off is between six and seven. And we've got to get the tree in then and a bit of something to eat too. And if we have to wait a minute after six to open the doors and let those children see the tree I don't believe even your father will be able to hold them in. I've got to sort all these presents and find the places for your plates. And just how we are going to get through I don't see. Seems if, no matter how far ahead you plan it, Christmas comes out this way after all—leastways if you keep Christmas at all," she amended, the memory of previously barrenly unhurried holidays making her pause. She passed feverishly to a mass of bundles of all sorts and shapes, some tissue-paper wrapped and gayly labeled, some clumsily done up by childish fingers in paper in which packages had come from the shops and stragglingly marked in pencil.

"Can't I help?" Helen was surprised herself when she found that she was coming eagerly forward. "I never trimmed a tree—I was the youngest at home—but I'd love to."

"Why yes, thank you, Miss Standish," Emma accepted cheerfully. "That would be right smart of help. We are short-handed this year because neither Mr. Schnorren nor yet Hans can get away."

Miss Standish and Ludwig worked busily. The dignity of great years and much knowledge that had been oppressing the Senior for the last year dropped from her, as did the boy's shyness. They sounded surprisingly like two happy and excited children as they chattered over the pretty, shining things. There is no doubt there is some subtle intoxicant in the imprisoned fragrance of evergreen.

Miss Metcalf watched them with a faint smile on her face. She herself took no part in the activities beyond handing the others an occasional ornament as they asked her for it.

The early twilight fell. Greta reappeared with a large platter heaped with the round or crescent, star-shaped or heart-shaped cookies that no German Christmas tree would be complete without. They fell to work more hurriedly. The lull outside had existed for so long that they had forgotten the tempestuous pair. But now there came energetic kicking at the locked door.

"Oh, what will we do with them?" Emma for the first time showed signs of flurry. "If my husband could only come! He can always quiet them with a word. But he will not be here for half an hour yet."

"I'll go out and keep them quiet," said Greta. "Miss Standish is quicker than I am anyway." And the cleverest girl in her class was obviously elated at the compliment.

It wanted but a quarter of an hour to the time when Father would return when a loud thump was heard on the floor of the room overhead, followed by a chorus of wails.

Crying, "My baby! He has fallen from the crib again!"

Unnoticed by the others Miss Metcalf stole after her. When the chemistry instructor reached the bedroom she found the baby gurgling, his fright forgotten, his bumps all healed with kisses. Emma was feverishly trying to dress the chuckling, wriggling rascal as well as she could for warding off the attention of the newly awakened twins.

"Oh dear, I really don't know how I *am* going to manage," Emma confessed, visibly flustered.

"Just let me stay up here with the children until you finish," suggested Miss Metcalf quietly.

Mrs. Schnorren gave her a surprised and dubious glance.

"The baby will come to me," said the college woman defensively. She held out her arms. Sure enough, the baby gave not so much as a look of inquiry before he jumped up and down in sign of consent. "Just go on. I'll manage them all."

And Mrs. Schnorren, feeling as though a snowbank had suddenly grown a hedge of wild roses, departed, thankful but confused.

Minutes passed. Noises multiplied themselves in the little house. Doors banged, the shrill voices of Tony and Clarchen were heard, deeper ones rumbled. Greta called loudly from somewhere for more twine, steps ran upstairs and clattered down—there was a lull; a new, deep voice sounded, followed by peals of laughter. Still Miss Metcalf was in the quiet chamber, shut up with the little ones.

At last Greta ran excitedly up to tell her that Father had come and that Christmas was going to begin. Downstairs they found a hobbling, exultant, babbling procession forming. The entry was all too small; the family stretched out into the dining room.

"The mother first, because she iss of us all the queen," Schnorren was saying. He was a short, red faced, jolly man, with not one spear of hair decking pate or eyebrow. At that moment he was doffing his smeared butcher's apron for his Sunday coat that his wife held ready. If Miss Metcalf had met him in the street he would have seemed to her a farcical figure, she reflected. Yet here, when he spoke, everything halted. "Then will Ludwig come so that he may lead the singing with his fiddle—— ."

"There's the baby!" called out Emma, her voice shrill with excitement.

Schnorren gave a genial, careless glance at this stranger who came down the steps with his baby. He knew nothing of her; Emma had no time to tell. But as he reached to take the baby from her arms he fancied that he caught a wistful look behind the glasses. He was probably mistaken, but sentiment rose easily in his bosom at christmastime. "Vill not this friend of ours herself the baby take in to see what the Christ-child has brought us?" he was impelled to say.

So escorted by the shining pated butcher, Miss Metcalf took her place. The rest lined up behind them; Greta, holding one round-eyed twin by the hand; Hans—such a short, important, red-cheeked, chubby little business man was Hans, carrying the other toddler. Tony and Clarchen, awed now and half dazed with excitement, could hardly be induced to take their places until their father's short command brought them there like little soldiers. Helen Standish lingered in the rear.

Schnorren threw open the door with a ceremonial flourish. Ludwig struck up a loud triumphant "Oh, Tannenbaum!" All of the voices were raised in a joyful chorus, wonderfully harmonious and musical. As the door showed them the glowing tree they slipped into the hushed, exquisite tenderness of *Heilige Nacht*. So the Schnorren household greeted with joy unspeakable their tree of joy.

It was not until the babel of voices exulting over gifts and goodies had risen to a most deafening medley, until everybody had laughed so hard that it would have seemed impossible to laugh any more, until the visitors had been forced to partake of sandwiches and coffee and *Kuchen* by Emma— overweeningly proud of being able to offer hospitality to her one-time patrons—until the base-burner had sent out waves of heat that made the small room fairly stifling and the pungent smell of evergreens could be almost distilled out of the air, that the unexpected guests roused themselves to remember that all this had not been in their program.

They made their way through the press with difficulty. The baby had—unfortunately perhaps—been taught to blow a piercing whistle; he was in full exercise of his new accomplishment, smiling seraphically and making a fiendish noise. Tony pounded deafeningly on a drum. Clarchen was jumping up and down, hugging herself and shrieking with all the joy of her untrammeled nature. Hans was beaming broadly over a new sweater. One twin was turning somersaults and the other had fallen asleep on he floor among his toys. And Greta was touchingly exultant over some real, grown-up kid gloves that she had hardly dared to hope for. It was evident that the joy of the Schnorren household was at its climax.

Then the visitors approached Emma, tired but content, enthroned on the hard, slippery sofa beside her complacent spouse. They said good-by.

It was Helen who burst out: "Emma, how wonderfully well you are looking!"

"Of course she is," Schnorren answered for her, taking his pipe out of his mouth. He regarded them with complacent masculine superiority. "She no longer so hardt has to vork," he said fatuously. "Too much of vork for all of us is badt. I vill not effer let my vife go out of the house the vork of other to do." His tone had become a warning one. Evidently Emma had told who they were and he thought they might have designs on his wife's super-abundant leisure.

The girls glanced at Emma. No inkling of any irony in the situation had penetrated. She had upon her face the preening smile of the pampered and protected wife. Still, when she had followed them hospitably to the door, Miss Metcalf at last put the question that had been haunting her.

Her tone was no longer sharp nor indignant. It was merely intensely curious:

"How is it, Emma, that with all this hard work, and the care, and the loss of your rest, you still have grown as you are, so wonderfully well and happy?"

Emma hesitated. She looked through the open door where Schnorren sat, with the baby cuddled in his arms. The language of sentiment did not come so easily to her as to that florid Teuton who had taken her to his heart and home. Her eyes mothered in turn each member of the little tribe to whom she was so necessary, whose hearts rested on her. She basked in the happiness of her little world—humble world though it might be, endlessly striving, its tiny prosperity so precarious, still the world that had enshrined her, hard-working, dutiful, hitherto unloved Emma, at the center of its warm beating heart. Her eyes returned to those who questioned her. There was something dumb in her eyes, and patient; they seemed to beseech the two women to understand her; there was some fear, perhaps, that they would smile. But all she said was:

"I don't know. Perhaps I do work hard—only somehow I never think of it that way. Work doesn't seem to tire me as it used to do. I guess it's because it's kind of—all right—here."

Her work-coarsened hand touched, with a gesture of surprising beauty and dignity, the gingham—she had not had time to change her dress for the festivities—that was stretched rather tightly over her heart.

The two young women had walked some squares in silence when Helen suddenly halted and faced Miss Metcalf.

"Charlotte, I know I'm going to disappoint you horribly and spoil the evening for you. But I can't help it. I'm not going to the theater. I—don't feel like hearing Shaw tonight. He's all right for some moods, but there are things—like Emma—that he doesn't understand. He's got a blind spot. And—oh, I'm homesick! I suppose that's what it means. I'm homesick for my own people, and their loving me, and the neighbors coming in, and the Christmas greens. I suppose I'm nothing but a baby after all, and you'll never respect me again. But I'm going straight out to the College and pack, and I can catch the six-thirty tomorrow morning and be at home for dinner. I'll telegraph at the station. I just haven't got any strength in me. I want to be with my own people, and—well, yes—with Jack!"

It was almost midnight when Miss Metcalf, looking up from a letter she was writing, saw Helen standing at the door. The girl stood straight and tall, trim and tailored, in the gown she would wear the next morning for her journey! Her eyes sought the older woman's humbly.

"You never said a word all the way coming out, Charlotte. Won't you forgive me? Indeed, I'm ashamed of myself. But I couldn't help it. I do love you, but——"

Miss Metcalf gave a low laugh and pulled the girl down on the couch beside her. And then Helen noticed that she looked as Miss Metcalf had

"'I Telegraphed Him——' 'Him? Who? Not Jack!'"

never looked before. Whether it was because of the pale blue dressing gown, or because her hair had tumbled into the softest knot almost on her shoulders, with the wavy lovelocks covering her high, fine forehead, or whether it was because her glasses had fallen off and so the sweet and tender mouth for once had its whole beguiling way—but anyway she was entirely different, and soft and kissable and huggable to a degree that made Helen's mind immediately ask itself the startled query: "Why isn't there some one———"

As if in answer Charlotte snuggled her head against the other girl's shoulder. "I telegraphed him———"

"Him? Who? Not Jack!" gasped the dazed Helen.

Charlotte laughed again with soft enchantment. "Oh, just the one absolutely splendid and perfect man in the world, of course. Only his name isn't Jack. It's an entirely different name. It's Jim. And I'm not going to him, because I haven't any home until I make him one. But he is on his way to me now, if I know him. Oh, Helen, Helen! I've been fighting him off for three interminable years. He was in my university: Only one year ahead of me. And I'm earning almost as much now as he does—even if in ten years he'll be miles ahead of me. That's the way it goes, you know, between trained men and women. But I was a coward and I was afraid of the ten years—the little house—the struggling—sordidness—being crowded—cabbage!" Here was I, I said, in my cool, secure, dignified comfort. What folly to give it all up even if——— But now—I know—I *know*. Of course it was that blessed Emma taught me. And—I never knew it was such an adorable thing to kiss a baby's neck—just below the ear—the sweetest spot———"

She turned suddenly on Helen and raised an admonitory finger. "I tell you, there's too much in me—I'm too much a woman to be wasted this way!" Her voice was argumentative, combative. "I've thrown myself away on you—little—priggish—schoolgirls!" she took the sting out of her words by a laughing hug that nearly took Helen's breath away. "I tell you a real man wants me!"

Her voice shook and she hid her face against Helen's boyish shoulder. Helen felt the tears moist against her cheek and she patted the face tenderly. Then the flushed face showed itself, the eyes alight with fun. The difference in their years? They were just two untried girls together, who listened to each other mainly because each in turn wanted an audience for her own confidences. The glorious instructor was, if anything, the more absolute a baby.

"I'd *love* a little house—and—if Emma can feel *that* way about a man who hasn't a spear of hair on his head, I fancy I can keep it up for Jim. And—the instructor in domestic science says there is an odorless way of cooking cabbage!"

FIVE

A Debatable Figure

LIKE THE MAGI, the lives of Charlotte Metcalf and her adoring student were changed by a child. Visitors from a world of privilege to a humble abode, they were converted at the "shrine" of a poor but charismatic infant. The connection between these young heroines of the December issue and those long ago kings could not have been an accident; the story was redolent with Christian symbolism. But Margarita Spalding Gerry's metaphors went far beyond the biblical. Her sentimental Yuletide confection, accompanied by two pictures that placed cherubic youngsters in the foreground, was designed to elicit warm thoughts of family life, emotions not only appropriate to the season but to the author's assertion that, for women, true fulfillment lies in motherhood and homemaking.

"The Woman Who Threw Herself Away," like much of the fiction published in the *Journal*, was designed to instruct as well as to entertain. But reading Gerry's story today, one is struck by the inconsistencies of its message. Despite the emphasis on the coldness of the academy, for example, there is ample evidence that hot passion (in the form of "crushes") warmed its otherwise chilly corridors. Moreover, if Charlotte Metcalf's soft, curly hair only veiled her "keen" intelligence, how comfortable would she find the discipline of marriage? And most important for the purposes of this analysis, even as Gerry paraded the joys of motherhood, her description made absolutely clear that she regarded the life of a single professional woman as far more attractive. It is here, in the easy acceptance of what seem to be obvious contradictions, that one discovers the spinster in her all too brief moment of ascendancy.

Gerry created two unmarried heroines who were far more beautiful, charming, and powerful than their married acquaintance. The demonstrable superiority of their lives reflected Gerry's view that single women led lives of high appeal. Indeed, her contrasting descriptions of existence in the college precincts and in Emma's house emphasized the privileges of the former and the burdens of the latter. Moreover, in her enumeration of the sacrifices that marriage and motherhood entailed, she endorsed the notion that single professional women enjoyed substantial intellectual, financial, and status advantages. Nonetheless, Gerry's rendering of single women—as physically, socially, and materially better off than their married sisters—did not entirely undercut the message that she so obviously aimed at purveying. Rather, in keeping with Christian tradition, by detailing the sacrifices that women made in marrying, she emphasized the redemptive possibilities of that estate.

Still, woman was not, at least in this version of the story, to be saved by wedlock alone. Maternity (embodied in the image of the Madonna) as opposed to marriage (embodied in the image of Eve) was proffered here as a precondition for change. Thus, it was caring for the butcher's children rather than marriage to the butcher that transformed the formerly gaunt and taciturn Emma into "a broad, rosy person and a surprisingly 'comfortable' hostess."

On one level, then, the message is clear. If motherhood served as the forge for the refinement and tempering of Emma's womanly qualities, how could it do less for the lovely and talented Miss Metcalf whose first name is only spoken awkwardly, and who has merely the unsatisfying attentions of her "crushes" for company? And if the "hard features" of a former servant could be softened by exposure to children, wouldn't domestic bliss accomplish even more for a woman already endowed with a "softly red and tenderly sweet" mouth? Surely it would beautify and feminize her "hygienically exercised, modern" and "boyish" young follower, Helen Standish.

More, the author implies, there may be some women who are naturally suited to the monastic life (though we are not actually introduced to any in this piece). But assuredly, a woman whose cool, austere demeanor is contradicted by soft, sweet features could not be among them. Or might she?

Had she lived, Rebekah Spofford would have been approximately fifty years old when the beautiful Miss Metcalf and her faithful and adoring student journeyed from the comfort of their college to one of the poorer quarters of the city. Much had changed in that quarter century. Single women had come to occupy an important position in the American imagination precisely because they illustrated the possibilities for female autonomy and accomplishment. Hewitt depicted Rebekah as a pioneer in ideas, career, and lifestyle. In contrast, by 1913, Gerry viewed female professionals as so well established that neither Miss Metcalf nor Helen had to struggle against family claims or social expectations. And they appeared to face no impediment to entry into the professorate. The beneficiaries of a dramatically expanded opportunity structure, Gerry's heroines not only represented all the attributes of feminine success, their lineaments described them as having realized the highest and most attractive capacities of "respectable" womanhood.

This was certainly no fiction. Between the late nineteenth century and the beginning of World War I, women not only established themselves within a set of new professions, such as social work, teaching, librarianship, and nursing, they also gained access to many of the previously all-male professions. The possibilities for self-support had expanded exponentially, and in some fields, most notably medicine and the professorate, women actually had higher levels of participation between 1910 and 1930 than in 1950.[1] As a much cited study of women and higher education by Patricia Albjerg Graham documented, the proportion of doctorates granted to women in the United States increased steadily until 1930 (reaching a ratio of close to one out of five), but by 1950 the proportion had declined to one out of ten. In fact, Graham's work, a landmark piece in the field of women's studies, led to a revision of the assumption that there had been "a progressive improvement in occupational possibilities for all segments of American society." Her analysis led her to conclude that "opportunities for highly educated women" actually may have been "greater at the end of the 19th century than they were in the mid-twentieth century."[2]

Professional opportunities were not available to all women, however. First of all, professional access was generally limited to a relatively privileged group—those who had access to extended education—generally, the daughters of the native-born middling classes. Barbara Solomon documented this phenomenon in her book on women in higher education, showing that women approached parity with their brothers in access to advanced schooling in this period. By 1900, more than one out of three college students were women and the representation of women on college campuses continued to grow, reaching 40 percent in 1910 and 47 percent by 1920 when the upward trend was reversed.[3] Second, and perhaps even more important, as a number of prominent scholars have noted, the entry of women into professional careers was, in fact, both tied to and limited to spinsterhood as a distinct life option. Women like Helen Standish and Charlotte Metcalf exemplified a new way of life. Before their conversion, they were preparing for lives of independence and self-fulfillment. But that existence required that they avoid marrying.

Gerry's presumption that a woman had to give up her occupation in order to marry reflected a general understanding. Access to college offered women the opportunity to prepare for professional life and promulgated the idea that they should be free to pursue careers. But while early collegians were offered many examples of intellectual and professional aspiration for women, they were also taught to see family and profession as incompatible options. Indeed, the most obvious exemplars of female achievement in fiction, as well as on college campuses—women faculty—were almost all unmarried.[4] Thus, on the one hand, while the joint expansion of higher education and career opportunities for women made it possible "for a woman to approach singlehood in a new way,"[5] Gerry's story dramatized the need to make a choice between marriage and career.[6] The premise—marriage alienated women's professional self.

The desire for independence may have led some women to eschew marriage; women who aspired to careers had little choice. The responsibilities of married life were clearly deemed inimical to professional accomplishment. In fact, it is no exaggeration to say that the career woman generally was an unmarried one. Perhaps as a result of cultural expectations or because of the high proportion of never-marrying women, the jobs that opened to women after the Civil War were mainly available to women who couldn't or wouldn't marry. As one historian has baldly asserted: "If a woman wanted a career she had to forgo marriage."[7] Thus, in her well-known study of American women in academia, Jesse Bernard noted that only single women had real access to the American professorate for most of the first half of this century—a qualification that was, apparently, similarly relevant for other professions.

Thus, although higher education offered women entry into professional occupations in the decades between 1890 and World War I, marriage was difficult, if not impossible, for career women. During the early part of the century, the sanctions against married women's employment in professional fields were so substantial that, with the exception of a few fields of private practice in which small female specialties were established, professional women were largely unmarried.[8] Neither was the taboo against married women limited to the male-dominated professions. The 1910 census reported that only 12 percent of women in all the various professions (including the "semiprofessions") were currently wed. In fact, married women were even less likely to gain employment in the female-dominated, largely salaried professions like school teaching than in fee-paying professions like medicine.[9] Marriage "bars" or formal bans against the employment of married women were commonplace, especially for teachers, from the late 1800s through the 1940s.[10]

The aspirations of head and heart were generally represented as incompatible in this period. Then as now, postulating the existence of a conflict between women's professional and family lives could hardly be called idiosyncratic but, in Gerry's day, heroines had to choose between them. And she, like many of her contemporaries, assumed that the aspirations and expectations of female collegians were raised by their sojourn in college and thus rendered them predisposed to embrace career over marriage. In fact, the collegiate experience was assumed to be so liberating that some early critics argued that colleges rendered women unfit to marry.[11] Certainly, the *Journal's* descriptions of college maidens in this period almost inevitably accepted that professional life had greater drawing power than domesticity.

So, even as she insisted on the joys of motherhood, like many of her contemporaries Gerry emphasized its burdens and difficulties. Perhaps for that reason, she depicted women as losing status when they entered wedlock. Emma, although a college servant, was poised to rise in the world until her marriage—to an immigrant tradesman—definitively placed her among the lower ranks of society. And her academic friends, Miss Metcalf and Helen, remained her superiors only so long as they also retained their single status. Charlotte Metcalf's epiphany might have propelled her into a more blessed and emotionally satisfying way of life, but it also involved, as she herself so ungracefully observed, shutting "the door of opportunity in her own face." Giving up her profession, even one that did not pay a woman as well as a man, entailed considerable sacrifice of money, comfort, and ease. It also required that she engage herself to "slave as she had never done before." Recipes for odorless cabbage would do little to mitigate the hardships of reduced circumstances and what was obviously a descent in lifestyle.

Yet while Gerry clearly intended to suggest that the spinster's path was lonely and less fulfilling in the taking than in anticipation and she obviously wanted to weigh in on the side of marriage, she exhibited little more faith in the erotic drawing power of men than did Hewitt. Rather, both she and her heroines held that those women who remained single in order to follow a profession enjoyed more benefits than those who married did. And more, they clearly thought that a woman electing to pursue a vocation did not necessarily have to give up on romance. Helen, for example, seems to have been attracted to the life of a single, professional woman as much by her love for her "uplifting" mentor as by her passion for learning.

Perhaps that is why Helen is described as having been masculinized as well as diverted from traditional womanly engagements by higher education. Remade her in dress and physical appearance, through exercise and exposure to college mores, she has become "boyish" in manner. And when we are given access to Helen's inner thoughts, we learn that she has learned to ignore any inner prompting that would lead to marriage. In fact, the graphic images that accompanied the story as well as the written text reinforce fleeting references to the prevalence of romantic passion inside a woman's college. It is surely significant that in one of the four drawings for the story two young women are depicted sitting on the edge of a bed with their arms around each other.

Although Gerry portrays Miss Metcalf as unfulfilled by what we now would regard as unmistakably homosexual advances, heterosexual desire—in the person of the (presumably) attractive suitors Jack and Jim—had not been sufficient for her heroines in the past. Helen, after all, was prepared to give up her lover to embrace chemistry and although Charlotte Metcalf says her Jim is "a real man" with hair, she dwells rather longer on the poverty and struggles that lie in wait for her if she marries him than on his attractions. Moreover, the men that these two women eventually decide to marry are never made flesh; they are important less for their personal qualities than because they provide the protagonists with the opportunity to marry. Indeed, the one man who is described in detail, Emma's husband, is certainly not a figure likely to incline a young woman toward marriage. Although he is certainly less objectionable than farmer Kittredge, he is "farcical" at worst and unimportant at best.

Gerry was not alone in expressing her suspicion that women were likely to find the single life more attractive than domesticity. In her analysis of the *Journal*'s attitude toward paid work for married women, Jennifer Scanlon concluded that

Many feared that economically independent women might abandon men and marriage. While the *Journal* and other sources argued the primacy of marriage in women's lives, they also often seemed to suggest that economic dependence was the only thing preventing women from abandoning these relationships.[12]

And if married women's economic independence presented a threat to the social order, how much more of a danger was the potential for a widespread female refusal to enter into wedlock in the first place?

That potent capacity for self-development and marriage refusal moved spinsters to the center of an ongoing series of debates about the character and future of family life in the United States. The preeminent representatives of female emancipation, spinsters epitomized a set of insurgent possibilities. They had become a sign and symbol of change for those who advocated as well as those who abhorred the idea of increased rights and liberties for women. Defined by their freedom on the one hand and by their accomplishments on the other, spinster visages were emblazoned on the standards of those who opposed, as well as those who advocated, women's independence. As a result, invocations of the never-marrying woman functioned as a kind of cultural switch, a rhetorical device that could be employed for a variety of social commentaries and moral purposes. The eminently respectable version of the "public woman," the never-marrying woman might be invoked either as an example of civic virtue, abhorrent possibility, or figure of fun.

Certainly, by 1913, the *Journal*'s editor had become so worried about what he saw as the seductions of the single life that he made his magazine a willing participant in an ongoing campaign to keep women in the family. Never doubting that spinsterhood was an enticing option, he was convinced that hordes of young women were disposed to avoid wedlock. And that, he thought, presented a clear and present danger to the future of the family.

Yet notwithstanding Edward Bok's numerous statements that men and women were meant to marry and that motherhood was women's highest calling, the magazine's content reflected a generally positive and sometimes adoring, if often concerned, view of women who never married. Year after year, in stories, columns, and editorials, those who elected for permanent maidenhood over wedlock (and there was never any hint that never-married women could be anything but celibate) were described, discussed, and often applauded. And even the magazine's attacks were mounted mainly to counter the seductive effects of spinster's accomplishments rather than to present them as defective in any way.

This was not what I had expected to find and certainly does not accord with what others have seen. In particular, this reading puts me somewhat at odds with at least one other set of analysts of the magazine's content. Patricia Searles and Janet Mickish have argued that it was the least supportive of nondomestic female roles of all the women's magazines. Analyzing the fiction published in the magazine during one year (1905), these scholars saw only conventional images of women projected. In their reading, they found that the *Journal*

> subtly . . . discouraged any social change that would alter . . . [the] idealized status [of wives and mothers] [and saw] independence and careers . . . as undesirable if not impossible for women.[13]

To the contrary, I think the *Journal's* "line" was far less consistent than Searles and Mickish suggest and that, as with Gerry's piece, the magazine's treatment of unmarried women effectively undermined as well as supported "conventionality."

That is not to say that in this period the "old maid" was always lauded in the magazine. But the general tone of the coverage accorded them supported positive imagery of that estate and furnished, however unintentionally, a nondomestic alternative for women. The *Journal's* attitude is particularly interesting in the context of growing public attacks on single women.

So, on the one hand, although the *Journal* cannot, by any stretch of the imagination, be described as the *Ms.* magazine of the past, it consistently voiced approval of women who eschewed marriage and family in order to devote themselves to some other calling. And while Bok was certainly not sympathetic to demands for radical change in male/female relationships, he and his contributors repeatedly presented the unmarried professional woman as an admirable, even compelling figure. Lauding her capacity for public as well as private service, they celebrated the emergence of the autonomous woman.

Indeed, there was hardly been a month in the years between 1890 and the appearance of Gerry's story when a spinster did not make at least a cameo appearance in the *Ladies' Home Journal*. Unmarried women were rarely lampooned even when, as was sometimes the case, they were regarded with dismay; they were far more likely to be portrayed as admirable, attractive, and even alluring than to be depicted as unattractive, foolish, or limited. Given Bok's acceptance of the view that single women were seductively attractive, it is not surprising that the *Journal's* editor reacted to what he saw as the growing number of single women with deep concern. He was clearly one of those who feared what Carroll Smith-Rosenberg describes as the effects of personal and economic female autonomy.[14]

Spinsters were often described in the *Journal* as followers of an alternate path to womanhood. As one contributor wrote in 1893:

> Royal womanliness is reached by a double highway—motherhood and spinsterhood—the first beautiful by nature, the second by a self-abnegation unmatched in the human family.[15]

In this construction, women faced bifurcated possibilities. Marriage and career were incompatible and the contentions of many of the "prominent feminist leaders" that they could be conjoined were considered untenable.[16] Indeed, the *Journal* accorded women the right of professional purpose only if they were willing to refrain from marriage and motherhood. In the magazine's view, a woman was only entitled to take the alternate path if she could convince herself and others her difference from the rest of her sex.

Persuaded that the numbers of women electing to remain single were growing too large, Bok expressed repeated concerns that marriage had been rendered unattractive by comparison to the alternative, even as he celebrated the accomplishments of unmarried women.[17] His concerns were substantial enough that by 1893, he had begun to rail against the dangerous influence of career women in his editorials. Complaining that the false allure of the "business" career undermined the family, he opined that young women might be seduced into abandoning their families and avoiding marriage altogether. As he put it, the "kind of girl" who "is tired of her dull home life . . . and [who] seeks independence . . . wants to . . . breathe the freer spirit . . . that a business career insures. . . . Upon this type of girl has much evil been wrought."[18] Magnified a thousandfold, such desires would spell disaster. If the most capable of young women opted out of marriage and childbearing, what would happen to the human race?

So while he applauded the accomplishments of single women and furthered their cause with encomiums about their worthiness and social importance, Bok also argued that marriage ought to be the main highway for adult women. In effect, he wanted the alternate course to be refashioned from a highway into a defile.

Given his ambivalence, it is not surprising that pieces defending and celebrating women who traveled the second "highway" were accompanied by others that stressed the difficulties that awaited those who embarked on that road. So, at the same moment that the *Journal* featured articles that were supportive of ambitious female aspirations, it also ran descriptions of the financial difficulties of women who eschewed marriage, the miseries that lay in wait for those who turned their backs on connubiality, and the lonely old age accruing to women who failed to reproduce. In the editorial pages and in the long-running feature, Ruth Ashmore's "Side-Talks With Girls," the *Journal* worked to discourage young women from responding to what she described as the falsely seductive attractiveness of a career in business. Several of the "Side-Talk" columns included lengthy descriptions of the financial and physical difficulties that working women might encounter. Bok also delivered frequent editorial panegyrics about the social importance of the home and the necessity for women to devote themselves to domesticity, especially those fortunate young women who had been to college.

In this vein, in one of an 1893 series of articles called "The Girl Who Goes to College," Anna Robertson Brown laid out a series of appropriate activities, demeanors, and expectations for "a girl . . . after graduating." Describing the benefits that college-educated women might bring to their homes, families, and communities, however, Brown lingered over the unhappiness that often followed the return home. She was very clear about the source of discontent—the contrast between the narrow sphere of domesticity and the heady, intellectual, and satisfying environment of college life. This author clearly perceived some propensity among college-educated women to despise and even turn against domesticity. Warning against "pride," "alarming" earnestness, display of "intimidating" learnedness, "selfish isolation," and "eccentric" behavior, she enjoined the new graduate to "prepare for marriage" by making "every day in your life . . . a bridal adornment . . . with the ornament of a lovely spirit, with the beauty of a gradually disciplined soul that has learned to meet life quietly and with courage, to do its duty without rub, or jar, or fret, and to adjust its strength for daily needs." In this

piece, Brown prefigured Gerry's argument. Celebrating the domestic potential of educated women, she also elaborated the problematic of the return
home. But her enjoinders to humility, like Gerry's references to sacrificial
purification, suggest that resistance to the yoke of family requirements was
not unheard of, and that some dissatisfied graduates might look for remedies
to their plight elsewhere.

Bok's concerns about the attractions of the single life seem to have
increased over time. Even as the *Journal* continued to applaud both the colleges
and their effects, concerns about the unwillingness of college-educated women
to cling to the hearth surfaced more frequently and, as the new century began,
the magazine increased its emphases on the superior virtues of domesticity. In
April 1903, for example, Bok's editorial "The College and the Stove" advocated the introduction of domestic science course into the required curricu-
lum of every "girls college." He argued that such an innovation would produce
several desirable results: it would teach students to better care for themselves
and improve their health; it would elevate the practice of housework and make
it more attractive to educated women; and it would help to solve the problem
of a diminishing supply of servants.

Whatever concerns Bok had about women abandoning family life,
however, career-minded college-educated women who did not marry were
rarely denigrated even by those who held some fears about their propensities
toward selfishness or eccentricity. On the contrary, continued references to
the attractions of the single life and the benefits that accrued to college-
educated women who turned their backs on marriage undermined their
intended message.

In February 1913, for example, a regular columnist for the *Journal*
named Edward Martin commented negatively on a speech delivered by
equality advocate Martha Carey Thomas, the president of Bryn Mawr
College.[19] Martin not only argued against suffrage for women, he applauded
the existence of rules preventing the employment of married women. Invoking the argument that women who wanted careers had to be willing to
accept spinsterhood as their lot, he contended that marriage was sufficient
employment to content most women. He said,

> not all women teachers or professors will regard as a "horrible
> alternative" a marriage, acceptable in other respects, which di-
> verts them from teaching and research and earning salaries. If a

woman is willing to marry a man at all she will usually be willing to live on his earnings, provided he can earn enough, and sometimes even when he can't. The women teachers and professors are not all so in love with their work that married life without it looks "horrible" to them. Some of them are delighted at the prospect of being relieved from wage-earning and of having a home, a husband and a family. I have known of such cases. . . . The fault, as I see it, that is to be found with [the unrest described by President Martha Carey Thomas of Bryn Mawr] . . . is that it overvalues independence for women, overvalues the wage-earning, untrammeled career, and undervalues the career that goes with marriage and domestic life.

Martin's eulogy on domesticity thus granted the very premises of the argument that it was incommensurable with independence, and suggested that women might feel themselves required to sacrifice more to have a family than to do without one. So even though many love stories appeared in the *Journal's* pages, love was not often invoked as an antidote to career-mindedness in this period, even by those who deplored what they saw as a tendency of women to abandon the family. The prospects of romance and passion were, apparently, insufficient to lure professionally inclined women into domestic responsibility.

The magazine's attitude reflects the fact that the spinster had become the representative of what historian Glenna Matthews terms the "respectable public woman." Until the late nineteenth century, Matthews contends, it was "literally inconceivable" to invoke " 'public woman' in a positive way, because there was no language to describe so anomalous a creature." She notes that the term "public woman" meant "prostitute" and was used as "an epithet for one who was seen as the dregs of society, vile, [and] unclean," while the male counterpart, "the 'public man,' represented a highly valued ideal." However, when a substantial number of women were able to find gainful employment outside the home *and* were able to earn sufficient money to live outside the home, "a woman's politics could be predicated on a basis other than domesticity."[20]

But precisely because of the broad possibilities open to the woman who remained unmarried in this period, this imagery came to carry substantial symbolic and emotional freight. It did not matter why she remained single and celibate, the spinster embodied freedom precisely because she was not obligated to others; she had turned her back on the "commonplace" and was not confined by the demands that were seen to prevent and protect women from singular action. Indeed, such women may have represented exotic but nonetheless alluring possibilities to readers precisely because their lives both defied and partook of the everyday round. Looking at the images of spinsterhood purveyed in the *Journal*, we can see alternate as well as normative constructions that may well have facilitated the development of insurgent self-conceptions; mirroring themselves in her portrait, women might envision nondomestic as well as domestic lives for themselves.

In Gerry's tale as in many others of the period, female denizens of the ivory tower were offered as exemplars of professional aspiration and accomplishment. Privileged beyond any expectations of prior generations, college women of 1913 embodied the best hopes and worst fears of their elders. Situated on the brink of adulthood and life decisions and, at the same time, enjoying a far wider range of options than most of their contemporaries, their actions could be taken as a clear sign of what it was that women wanted. They were, in short, ideal subjects for any discussion about the vexing "woman question."

At the turn of the century, unmarried women figured large in the minds of those who aimed at opening the world for female advancement as well as those who aimed at keeping women safely confined in a revivified family. Spinster iconography was, in consequence, contested territory. Advocates of female advancement may have embraced the accomplishments of women who devoted themselves to the human family at large, but others warned of dire consequences if women were encouraged to abandon the domestic realm. So, even though "singleness" was depicted as a concomitant element of female independence, careers for women could easily be perceived either as substitutes for or alternatives to marriage and the services rendered by professional women could be defined either as an extension or subversion of devotion to family and children.[21]

Perhaps the spinster was most open to attack in this, her finest hour. For some, she became the most egregious actor in what was conceived to be a national tragedy—the abandonment of family and family life by the very backbone of advanced and civilized society. Thus, even as women who eschewed marriage were extolled and applauded as the incarnation of female accomplishment, they were also denounced as a danger to the persistence and stability of family, nation, and race. A number of prominent citizens, convinced by the eugenicist emphasis on "racial" distinctiveness, saw declining rates of family formation and fertility among the native-born, Anglo-Protestant middle classes conjoined with high fertility levels among immigrant groups from southern and eastern Europe as a recipe for "race suicide." In this view, women's desire for independence could only lead to disaster, particularly as the women who were most likely to turn their backs on marriage and children in pursuit of careers were assumed to be the daughters of superior citizens. No less a figure than the president of the United States was galvanized by this specter. Theodore Roosevelt used the public visibility of his office, his "bully pulpit," to condemn the "viciousness, coldness, [and] shallow-heartedness" of those women of good "stock" who, avoided their "duty" to procreate the "race."[22] Yet increased emphasis on the necessity for marriage and reproduction was not directly connected to any real increases in the numbers of single women. Rather, it surfaced well after the time when the proportion of women who remained unmarried had peaked in the United States and even begun to level off.[23] Here as elsewhere, eugenics was invoked, as one historian put it,

> by modernizing elites to represent their prescriptive claims about social order as objective statements irrevocably grounded in the laws of nature [because] eugenics promoted a biologizing vision of society in which the reproductive rights of individuals were subordinated to the rights of an abstract organic collectivity.[24]

The debate over the future of the family was necessarily one that was joined within elite circles, the very groups that President Roosevelt excoriated as committing race suicide. Yet because the iconography of spinsterhood presumed middle- or upper-class status, representations of unmarried women served cultural purposes in working-class as well as bourgeois circles. So while elite attacks on unmarried women reflected "racialized" concerns about the broad possibilities open to women who remained unmarried, in representations directed to and consumed by working-class audiences ridicule of the "old maid" also became a way of lampooning the classes that produced her. This was especially the case for working-class audiences at burlesque performances, the popular entertainment form that Robert Allen describes as an "arena for 'acting out' cultural contradictions and . . .

contestations" through the "aesthetics of transgression, inversion, and the grotesque."[25] Here again, it was the combination of celibacy, status, and a claim to independence that defined the icon, but in this instance she was turned into a ludicrous figure.

In the burlesque halls, which rendered "take-offs on venerated objects of high culture" to working-class audiences,[26] the spinster was used as a standard figure of fun, a target for attacks on the middle classes. These slyly subversive representations in and for the working-class milieu were apparently among the most successful of the sharp and vitriolic forays against the upper classes that characterized the medium.[27] In some of the most noted of these performances, representations subsequently inscribed in the emerging medium of film, the "old maid" was displayed as a man masquerading in female garb.

Sharon Ullman has graphically described the phenomenon in her history of public sexual culture. She says that "the frustrated old maid" was a "dominant female stereotype" in films and that many male performers and, later, filmmakers "built their careers" on enacting these roles. Performed by men in drag, these parodies emphasized the unity of the type and the "potency of her ugliness." They employed what Ullman called "identical female imagery" in order to complete the comedic impression of "sexuality unused, and thus outside of communal control and direction," associating the rejection of heterosexuality with advocacy of women's rights. The "socially agreed-upon repudiation of a certain form of older single woman [who stood as] . . . an icon of unacceptability—repelled and repellant," was, according to Ullman, a response to the attempts of reformers (often educated middle-class women) to suppress working-class sexuality.[28]

Still, whether the spinster remained unwed and celibate by design or default, she embodied freedom. Precisely because she was not obligated to others and had turned her back on the "commonplace," she was not confined by the demands that were seen to prevent and protect women from singular action. In the main even as women gained entry into both older (formerly male) professions like medicine and academia, and into the rapidly expanding ranks of the new professions like social work, only women who remained unmarried were deemed "free" enough to take advantage of expanding horizons. Whereas both advocates and enemies of increased rights for women described the married woman as tied by husband, parturition, nurturance, and attendant domestic and emotional responsibilities, her unfettered spinster counterpart was seen as positioned to take full advantage of such new rights, liberties, and opportunities as became available.

At the same time, however, the woman who remained unmarried was used as a means of representing both threats to societal stability and the ridiculous embodiment of respectable middle-class femininity. In this manner, the spinster was more defined by her privileges and freedoms than by her domestic deficiencies. As a symbol of emancipation, and a sign of female possibility, spinsters were constituted almost as a unique group in which both sexual characteristics and gender expectations were mutable in the face of class privilege. In those media that targeted respectable middle-class women, it was inevitable that such an estate would be ambiguous.

There was one additional and consequential claim implicit in these accounts and that was that not every woman was capable of accomplishing spinsterhood. The "old maid" of 1890, for example, counterpoised her high sense of responsibility against the desire to cling to a "manly heart" as follows: "I never married because since I have been twenty-five years old, life has been full of so much that it seemed my duty to do, that I did not believe that marriage was the main part of my existence." "Not many women can drink this cup," another contributor contended, "but those who can find even its bitter a tonic piquant and strengthening."[29] "I was not willing to have my heart and brain shriveled and sucked dry," said the "Spinster Who Has Learned to Say No," implying that the common run of women were both less talented and discerning. One 1893 piece even went so far as to assert that

> a clever woman's 'gifts' have a disqualifying matrimonial tendency, the experience of the ugly duckling having its constant counterpart among [women endowed above the average. Their 'gifts' may excite admiration but they keep them at arm's length, popularity being rather the result of a happy development of commonplace qualities.[30]

Conversely, of course, only the unusually talented had the capacity to remain single—to aspire to a life beyond the domestic frontier. As one piece describing "The Happy Woman" asserted,

> There is occasionally born into the world a woman whose whole nature rushes like the tide of a mighty ocean toward the shore

of some especial career. Rosa Bonheur was one of these, the first Mrs. Siddons was another, Anna Dickinson was another. In each of these women the force of her peculiar genius was so great that no perfection of home life, no opulence of wealth, could have kept her from fulfilling her destiny. They did not choose a career, a career chose them.[31]

Of course, far from derogating spinsterhood, such pieces may well have had the effect of elevating it in the imagination. Even in Bok's most negative arguments, the single life was presented as an alluring alternative. How could it be otherwise, his jeremiads suggested, when the life of the woman of "business" was far more attractive than that of her less glamorous married sister. The linguistic portraits and accounts of never-marrying women that appeared in the magazine can be read as defining and elaborating the elements of the persona of these newly important figures. Editorials, features, news items, and stories depicted single businesswomen who had climbed the occupational ladder or were pointing the way to economic success. They also admiringly presented maiden ladies whose instinct for humanity led them to leave their own fireside to travel cross-country or put themselves forward in order to save the lives of strangers, care for desperate family members, or make a home for orphaned children. But the spinsters of this period were just as likely to possess intellectual abilities and talents that made it difficult for them to accommodate themselves to the requirements of a husband. In this way the magazine, its staff, and contributors not only gave unmarried women important roles in various life dramas, they took the opportunity to celebrate their accomplishments.

Of course, some number—perhaps the majority—of the real-life women who inspired this adulation were sexually active. Nonetheless, their public portraits rendered them chaste. They may, like Miss Metcalf and her acolytes, have engaged in episodic flirtations with members of their own or the opposite sex, but the explicit contrasts between their demeanor and that of working-class women like Emma Schnorren emphasized their middle-class propriety. And decent women, of course, did not engage in sex before marriage.

Spinsters came of age in those heady years when new opportunities opened for women, especially women who remained unmarried. In these years, the once commonplace, if sometimes comical figure of the past, the celibate and childless unmarried woman, found a new place in the cultural pantheon. Exemplifying (through retention of her maidenhead as well as her maiden name) the respectable alternative to domestic entanglements, she embodied the essence of female emancipation.

The attempt at redefinition opened up new possibilities for attacking women and their movement for political and social equality, reflecting what Arlene MacLeod refers to as the "immense difficulties of appropriating language for new and oppositional uses." Within constraints that offer few alternatives, she says, insurgents may seek to redefine traditional categories in a "symbolic struggle, a negotiation over meaning" that affects the possibilities for action. MacLeod suggests that such efforts may backfire because a given symbol may well maintain "a somewhat separate life of its own, carrying both intended and unintended messages."[32] In a similar vein, Yvonne Zylan cautions that structures of political opportunity may make it possible to mount insurgency by attempting to appropriate the linguistic weapons of those with cultural power, but that such battles are difficult to win because those who seek redefinition lack power to begin with.[33] Such was the case with the spinster; the claim that she represented freedom was not, as the next story shows, sustainable over the long run.

Six

"A Lady Scholar?"

DURING THE 1920s, college women emerged as "an important subject and target audience" for the *Journal*.[1] However, at least in the pages of this magazine, the normal college woman found professional life far less seductive than the attractions of love and marriage. So, in the 1933 story, "The Whip of Emotion," contrived by freelance writer Lois Montross, heterosexuality was assumed to be a much more powerful motivating force than career. In Montross's tale, Mary Carolyn Lowry, a psychology major, is attracted to the idea of becoming a professional woman and considers breaking up with her fiancé to pursue graduate studies. However, a whiff or two of the sexual abnormality involved in such a choice serves to dampen her enthusiasm for further study, moving her back on the path toward matrimony.

The Whip of Emotion
by Lois Montross, 1933

Although she wore rubber heels, Mary Carolyn fancied she heard herself stamping along the board walk that stretched across the campus clear from University Hall to Spencer. Under her breath she murmured plain and fancy curses. Behind her loitered the other nine students who were also transferred from Sebastian's class. She could hear them laughing and talking. They didn't care. They would have been surprised to know that she was furious.

"WHATEVER HAPPENS
YOU MUST REMEMBER
THAT I LOVE YOU. . . .
I LOVE YOU UNBE-
LIEVABLY"

The Whip of Emotion • • •   By LOIS MONTROSS

"What good is it," she asked herself, "to be a senior, to be known in every activity, to go to all the dances, to be chosen for the beauty section, to be fairly sure of Phi Beta. Ashes! Ashes!" she added with a gesture of such drama that she found herself smiling in spite of her bitterness.

She remembered that she was wearing Brent's fraternity pin. Nice Brent. They would be married next year. She tried to conjure the image of his frank, smooth face, his fine blond hair; but, unbidden, another image grew vivid in her memory, an extremely handsome face with dark amused eyes and a small pointed black beard. Professor Sebastian! How she hated him.

Now at the very door of Spencer Hall, where she was supposed to enter the new psychology quiz section, Mary Carolyn suddenly stopped and let the other students pass her. Then after a moment's thought she hurried to Dean Fannicott's office in the Administration Building. Other people thought him cold and obstinate, but Mary Carolyn had a way with Dean Fannicott. He often abetted her in unacademic procedures—dropping courses, reelecting them, entering advanced classes. He, unlike most other males, took her education seriously. Just because she was pretty he did not think her mind unimportant. . . . As Sebastian evidently did. Horrible Sebastian!

Fortunately she found the dean just unlocking his office. With his stiffly gallant bow, which seemed slightly mocking, that pale, precise man motioned her to a chair beside his desk. He placed his hat in the cupboard and planted his green baize bag of papers squarely upon the desk. "Now, what can I do for you, Miss Lowry? Not reelecting Birds again, I hope?"

The bird course had almost spelled disaster. The long morning tramps had seemed devastating when she was already overburdened by the dances and studies which evenly divided the kind of mad energy she had.

Her eyes sparkled toward his face and then clouded with gravity; magically she always knew when to mute the feminine note. She had been born with this trick. She often watched her instinct for it with detached respect. Without that gift no woman can be both intellectual and charming and she had no desire to be one or the other exclusively. To blend the two roles was her great, difficult, presumptuous aim. She was young. She was wrought of fire, humility and pride. To be Mary Carolyn Lowry gave her delight and trepidation. It was like soberly directing an inexperienced actress of natural genius. She escaped conceit because imagination swept her toward incredible goals.

"No," she said, "but, for the past two years, I've meant to take Psychology 18—Professor Sebastian, you know. Well, I registered for it and just now at the first class he said it was too crowded. He sent ten of us over to Miss Parmalee's quiz section."

Dean Fannicott raised his straight, severe eyebrows.

"Miss Parmalee is quite competent. Quite."

"But mediocre," said Mary Carolyn.

The dean regarded her thoughtfully. "Have you any reason for preferring Professor Sebastian?"

She cross-questioned herself. Had she any but silly reasons? Other women said he was fascinating. He was brilliant, good-looking, eccentric. His course was said to be exciting and unusual. But now the chief reason was that she hated him. At the first meeting of the class this semester he had glanced quickly around the crowded room. He was tall and thin and slightly stooped. His expression was inscrutable in spite of the dark, amused eyes. He had black hair and a black Vandyke, trimmed meticulously to a point which made his chin saturnine!

After calling the roll, he exclaimed, "Thirty Thirty!" He glanced about the room as if the students were guilty of a breach of etiquette. The women, who were in the majority, stirred with uneasiness. "I can't take care of more than twenty," he said. "I'll transfer ten of you to Miss Parmalee, whose section is still incomplete." Then he began reading names from his class roll. He did not do it alphabetically. He had amazingly glued names to faces in this first brief period. There were nine who rose, a bit awkward, but not caring enough to be really disgruntled. Mary Carolyn was complacent, for she had every right to believe that she was not the kind of dull student who makes life monotonous for the instructor. Her interest in psychology was serious, and as a senior she had found it inevitable to register for Sebastian's noted course.

As he gazed at the row in which Mary Carolyn sat she decided that her neighbor, a plump little blonde, would be added to the slaughter of the innocents. Professor Sebastian said: "And you, Miss_____? " Even the sudden failure of his extraordinary memory was affronting. "Lowry," she replied, feeling a flush rise on her cheek bones.

He couldn't mean her—he couldn't!

"And you, Miss Lowry," he said, singling her out with deliberation.

She followed the others from the room with the feeling of a Thoroughbred turned out to pasture with plow horses.

Now with every ounce of her determination she meant to return to Sebastian's class, because it would annoy him.

She told Dean Fannicott: "I read his book this summer with the expectation of knowing him personally this year."

The dean smiled cautiously. "If you were not such a good student, Miss Lowry, I might suspect you of the common motives which—uh—have led so many of our young ladies to sign for his course. However, knowing your interest to be purely academic—"

"Dean Fannicott," she began, "if you think——" Unexplainable tears rose to her eyes. Angry at herself for the weakness of vanity, she managed to add: "I've worked hard enough to deserve the choice of instructors. And if I think he's more—more—"

"More interesting?" asked the dean, ignoring the hint of tears, but obviously embarrassed.

"More valuable," she said in a small, rigid voice. She didn't care how much she had to praise him if only she could go back and somehow revenge herself.

"I'll see that you are not transferred," said the dean in a most business-like way.

II.

At four o'clock she met Brent in Harry's Hideaway, where lovers kept long, murmurous trysts in the narrow, dimly lighted booths, redolent of tobacco smoke and malted milk. She was proud of Brent's big muscular shoulders and the aggressive mold of his ruddy face. He would be gradu-ated from law school this spring and was confident of later passing his bar examinations. He was already planning the wedding; with enthusiasm for all social details he had chosen the best man and the ushers and many of the guests.

"You see," he said, squeezing her hand, "this isn't just a fraternity pin romance. It's love with a wedding ring. It isn't just moonlight; it means a home and partnership and mutual understanding."

"Love at high noon," said Mary Carolyn, "in a cutaway and gray striped trousers?"

"A bonded cupid," he told her, "with common sense in escrow."

"What if the little beast jumped the bond?" she asked.

"We'd still have our common sense to fall back on."

"Brent, what makes you think I have good sense? I know you have, and that's one reason I love you. I think we're all a little tired of nuttiness and gaga-ism. But I often think my own emotions aren't too well trained. They run away with me when I least expect it; and the psychologists tell us that——"

"Oh, psychologists!" Brent dismissed them with airy impatience.

"——that training the emotions is the last thing scholasticism can do for us. . . . For instance, today I was quite shocked at myself. Sebastian trans-ferred me to another section. And for no reason at all—for *absolutely* no reason, Brent—I was furious. I was actually up in arms! I rushed straight to Dean Fannicott and got myself transferred right back. . . . Now, why on earth did I care?"

"Oh, nerves," he averred without thought. "And you're so tired."

"I'm not tired! Brent, please, I hate to be told I'm tired. And psychology isn't so simple as all that."

Brent lit a cigarette. "Psychology," he said cheerfully, "is the bunk."

Mary Carolyn narrowed her beautiful eyes and stared at him. With the detached interest of a scientist she noted that her face grew hot, her pulse quickened, her tongue felt loosened, as if it might deluge the world with illogical words. She wanted, for instance, to retort that law was the bunk, and see how he liked that. But she resisted childishness and began to think; "Here I am furious for the second time this afternoon. And maybe he's really right in dragging nerves in by their ganglia. . . . But I'll be darned if I'll have nerves. At my age! No neurotics in the Lowry family."

Her tone was carefully gentle: "It's like any other science that's been popularized too much. What smattering the layman reads usually *is* the bunk."

"Whadd'ye mean—science?" demanded Brent. "They pretend to card-catalogue the brain cells. Science—phooey!"

Mary Carolyn tried so hard to restrain her voice that it quivered like a highly bred race horse.

"But they don't. That isn't modern. . . . We"—and now she proudly included herself among psychologists—"we try to explain human conduct in terms of brain cells."

"You might as well try to explain human conduct in terms of fishes; only we know more about fishes." Brent was enjoying himself. He was having a dandy time. He wasn't angry—even if she were to attack law he wouldn't be angry. Worst of all, he didn't know that Mary Carolyn was angry. Am I going to marry this hide-bound, insensitive brute? she wondered. But of course she was. His frank, smooth face, his good shoulders, his wide hands with thick blond hair showing candidly below the wrists. . . .

"For instance," she went on smoothly, "a psychologist could easily explain your enmity toward the subject."

"How?" He was surprised.

"Jealousy that I'm so interested in something apart from you."

"I'll be damned!" said Brent, disarmed and ingenuous. "I wonder if that really is the reason?" Then with sudden craftiness he inquired: "And how do you explain your rage when Sebastian transferred you?"

"Oh, that," she said, turning the tables on him, with a wit that had almost escaped her for an instant—"that is explained by nerves. You see, I'm so tired."

And yet that evening at her sorority's most important rushing party she found time to wonder if what really caused her angry preoccupation was Professor Sebastian. No doubt the psychologists would have a word for it But she could not think of the word much less spell it.

III.

On friday afternoon Mary Carolyn walked into Room 201, University Hall, just as Professor Sebastian was calling the roll. She was deliberately, calmly, tardy. She wore a red wool dress under her black leather jacket, and she had pulled—with careful carelessness a red beret over her smooth hair. Her white organdie collar and cuffs were tailored, her Windsor tie demure. She had spent the morning shopping at the best department store in the college town. She had pretended to herself that she really needed the red dress, so delightfully soft that it was called rabbit skin. She made an idle discovery that the softer the fabrics a woman wears, the more alluring she is, just as kittens and rabbits are fascinating because of their tender pelts. She saw now the reason why Brent had felt lukewarm about her gorgeous metal-brocade evening gown. "But I did like the old black velvet one," he had said regretfully. And he had held her politely and remotely while they were dancing.

As she entered Room 201, she was conscious of moving with the quietude and graciousness of an actress. Professor Sebastian glanced at her sharply and his black eyes were puzzled. But he did not say anything until after the class, when he detained her. "Just a moment, Miss—uh—"

"Lowry," she prompted coldly. She had read that repeatedly forgetting a name might indicate a subconscious dislike for the person.

"Didn't I transfer you to Miss Parmalee's section?"

"Yes." She had rehearsed her explanation many times. She didn't want it to flatter him. "But Dean Fannicott thinks I had better remain in yours."

"What on earth does he have to do with it?" asked Professor Sebastian rudely, crossly.

"He is my senior adviser." she was deliciously conscious of being alone in the quiet room with him. Red and brown leaves falling outside . . . the branches of a stripped elm tree tapping wistfully against the windowpane. But there was late sunlight which made a chased pattern of gold against the desk, against Sebastian's black hair and beard. She felt her own vanity slipping weakly, submissively before the compulsion of his amazing eyes. . . . All at once she wanted terribly to please him and she said: "Dean Fannicott thought your instruction would be more valuable."

Without smiling, he asked, "Are you a good student?"

"Yes," said Mary Carolyn. "Haven't you heard of me?"

"Only as a prom-trotter."

"I led the junior prom last year," she told him with an air of gentle meditation, "without forgetting the identity of Locke, Berkeley or Hume."

"I don't believe in the education of women," said Professor Sebastian.

"I believe in the education of men," said Mary Carolyn. "Especially their education in politeness."

"I don't want you in my class," he said. "I can't be bothered with beautiful young things in my class. They only make trouble."

"A psychologist could explain that attitude," said Mary Carolyn. "I am really a very good psychologist."

He looked as if he hated her. She had a wild exultance at meeting the dark enmity of his gaze. He was so aware of her that she would be stamped irrevocably on the cover of his mind's mysterious volume.

"Your guess is very glib," he objected, "and very wrong. The amateur calls every prejudice a repression. The word covers a multitude of grins."

"Then you're simply a woman hater?"

"No. That would be womanish. Women smother their intellects with emotion."

"And men mother their intellects with emotion," she said, feeling in the triumphant instant that she was nobody's fool.

As Mary Carolyn met his eyes steadfastly Sebastian moved away from the sunlight stroking his short beard with a white, nervous hand. "Perhaps you won't care to stay in my section now?" he asked hopefully.

"I do though," said Mary Carolyn. There was a moment of silence.

All at once his face relaxed into a boyish smile and he shook hands with her. "You're rather a good sport, you know."

After this fine truce she left the room and literally ran down the creaking, splintery stairs of Old University Hall. That evening when Brent came to take her to a Student Union dance he noticed an unusually luminous quality about her face, and her dark eyes were like misty candle flame.

"Get a check from home?" He asked in a prosaic voice which aroused her impatience.

"No, I had one Monday. And I've spent most of it already."

"You seem awfully happy. But somehow I don't think it's about us."

"It is!" she protested. Then slowly and honestly she added: "At least I *think* it is."

"Listen," said Brent: "Mr. Lewis Hitchcock, a friend of my father's, will take me into his law offices after I pass my bar examinations. Chicago. Would you like to live in Chicago? Or maybe I should say, would you mind living in Chicago?"

"I think," said Mary Carolyn, "that I'm going to apply for an assistant's job in psychology."

"O.K.," he replied. "You could try either at Northwestern or Chicago University."

"Oh, no!" she cried swiftly. "I wouldn't think of doing it anywhere but here."

They were walking to the Union Club along a wide tree-lined street, and their feet made a quick swishing sound in the fallen October leaves. When he stopped suddenly and stared at Mary Carolyn everything seemed very quiet in the pale chartreuse moonlight.

"Then that means a postponed wedding—and a postponed wedding is usually no wedding at all."

"Brent, how can you? It just means that I'm awfully serious about my work."

He laughed with odd, rough irony. All at once he put both arms around her slim waist and drew her face close into the hollow of his shoulder and she could hear his heart beating. "Whatever happens," he said, "you must remember that I love you. . . . I love you unbelievably," he added in a hoarse, unfamiliar voice.

Touched, she stood on tiptoe and raised her mouth to his devout kiss. But a secret channel of her mind seemed to flow on swiftly, untouched by this interlude. Several times while they were dancing she checked herself when she was about to describe the interview with Sebastian. She wanted very much to talk about that curious man. She tried to decry him, thinking, "I'll bet he can't dance and Brent dances so gloriously," and "Sebastian has white hands and thin shoulders. . . . Brent's hands are strong and brown and his shoulders are swell."

IV.

But when the second semester arrived with inexplicable fleetness, Mary Carolyn registered for Psychology 18B with an eagerness undisguised to herself. And this time Professor Sebastian angrily scanned a room crowded with forty students, most of them women. Immediately he began to call off the names of those he was consigning to the mediocre Miss Parmalee. The name of Mary Carolyn Lowry remained upon his class roll. As he finished the L's his eyes and hers exchanged a glance of secret amusement which brought them together in comradeship.

Very tall and imperative, he stood by the window as he explained the new routines of the second semester. Mary Carolyn noticed his new slim dark suit, and she reflected that in spite of his hard, superior mind he was not immune to the vanities which even a minor deity might possess. He must know, for instance, the effectiveness of his black eyes and black beard against the pallor of his skin. And when he turned his profile toward the window she thought of somber, burning medieval faces—Savonarola or Lorenzo de' Medici perhaps.

"I also want volunteers," he said, "for a little laboratory research on Saturday afternoons. It won't help you with your marks, to be sure, but it will help me a great deal in regard to an article I am writing. Any willing martyrs in this great cause stop at my desk after class."

Only two men volunteered, but there were eight women, among them Mary Carolyn. Rather mysteriously, without describing his purpose, he gave each a different time for the appointment, at half-hour intervals. The place was to be the top floor of University Hall, where Professor Sebastian and his assistants had a sanctum sanctorum, which also harbored rats, dogs and sometimes monkeys. "Be prompt," he cautioned them. "Leave curiosity at home and bring a calm, scientific mind."

Mary Carolyn lingered after the others. She had made a swift decision—made it impulsively under the spell of his fascination for her. "Professor Sebastian," she said, "I want to do assistant's work for you next year. I thought I'd better speak to you as soon as possible."

He smiled at her thoughtfully.

"My dear young lady," he said, "I've already had half a dozen applications."

Her face clouded. "All women I suppose."

He nodded a modest assent, but his eyes sparkled with amused satisfaction.

"You see," she told him recklessly, "they just did it because they are crazy about you. . . . You see I'm different. I'm crazy about psychology."

Was she wrong in thinking that he frowned, that his voice was cooler? "Dear me!" he said. "So you're really a lady scholar?"

"Haven't I proved it?"

"Your outside activities seem very frivolous."

"But I won't have any next year!" she replied eagerly. "I'll be a stodgy P. G. I'll be taking my master's, you see."

"How can a woman be both pretty and clever?" he demanded.

"How can a man be both handsome and brilliant?" Now she knew that he was pleased. A self-conscious flush rose to his cheeks, and he touched his beard lightly with his finger tips.

"It is easier for a man to drive his mind without the whip of emotion." Then he added with a quick pretense of brisk officialdom, "In the meantime see Dean Fannicott and fill out the proper form."

When Mary Carolyn left Spencer Hall she had a hollow sensation as if she were lost—it was almost like the homesickness she had during a visit to her aunt when a very little girl. She admitted the truth to herself, half in fear, half in relief. "I'm in love. . . . Mary Carolyn, do you realize that you're in love—with Professor Sebastian? . . . But I can't be. I'm going to marry Brent. . . . Of course you can't marry Brent—not when you care for Sebastian like this. Why did you have to? I think you must be crazy. . . . I know, but he's so wonderful. Oh, damn, damn! How shall I ever tell Brent?"

She saw Brent that night, but she was so merry and companionable that presumably he did not guess the leadenness of her heart. "I *must* tell him, I must," she kept prodding herself. Yet every time the words formed themselves in her mind her lips grew stiff and cold and she found them saying something funny that made him laugh uproariously. "One reason we love each other so much," he explained contentedly, "is because we laugh at the same things."

V.

In order to assist Professor Sebastian in his research, Mary Carolyn canceled a date with Brent to see a hockey game on Saturday afternoon. Yet she dressed much more carefully than if she had kept the date—she allowed herself the luxury of wearing a dark blue-green suit which was too sophisticated in cut for ordinary campus wear, and she added the pert little pancake hat with a tiny gray coque feather, and her lovely new Christmas furs of silvery fox. She dressed, in fact, as if she were going to a matinee or a tea in the city, and she excused herself by remembering that the appointment had nothing to do with class work.

The top floor of University Hall seemed large, dusty and mysterious. All the doors were closed. She walked twice around the corridors and decided, somewhat hesitantly, to rap on the door which had the most thumb prints.

A young man, very thin, solemn, and wearing bone-rimmed glasses, asked her to come in. She recognized him as the assistant who took the class roll at the psychology lectures or gathered the pink and blue examination books.

"Miss Lowry?" said the solemn young man.

"Yes, I hope I'm not late." She consulted her wrist watch negligently, adjusted the fox scarf about her round throat. She anticipated something interesting; probably she was going to be psychoanalyzed. She looked forward intensely to answering personally embarrassing questions. She could fancy the detachment with which Sebastian would ask them and she meant to reply with absolute honesty. Probably it would be one of those tests in which they shoot a word at you and you answer with another out of a clear subconscious sky. If he said "Worry," she would retort, "Brent!" If he said "love," she would answer, "You!" and then. . . . But the assistant was speaking; as he gave instructions he kept his eyes glued on a notebook in which he was carefully writing.

"Please go behind that screen," he said in a colorless voice, "and take off your outer clothes and put on the kimono which is hanging there on

Illustrated by Henry Raleigh

SEBASTIAN'S ARM DARTED BACKWARD AND IN A SECOND'S PARALY-
SIS OF UNBELIEF SHE SAW HIM FLICK A WHIP AT HER ANKLES.
TEARS STOOD IN HER EYES, BUT HIS FACE WAS STERN, IMMOBILE

a hook. Be sure to take off your shoes and stockings too. . . . Professor
Sebastian will see you as soon as you are ready."

Mary Carolyn went quickly behind a screen and found there a clean
but draggled Japanese kimono. She donned it after taking off her suit and

blouse; feeling more and more affronted she took off her shoes and stockings. She added some rouge and powder to her face and left her purse on the floor by her shoes because there was no other place to put it. As she emerged from behind the screen she noted a long mirror at the left of the door by which she had entered. She gasped angrily. In this cheap cotton kimono, barefoot and without any sure, bolstering mood, she looked awkward and cringing. She tried to drape the kimono about her hips in a more graceful fashion, but there was no way on earth to arrange it becomingly. If she held it at one place it bulged at others with a kind of bourgeois complacency. Her bare feet pressed flat against the hard wooden floor seemed astonishingly large, and even red; her face was marred by an unbecoming, self-abased expression. She reminded herself, in fact, of her mother's washerwoman. She moved forward, simply because she couldn't bear to confront her own unprepossessing image any longer.

At the same moment Professor Sebastian entered the room. The assistant, seated under the window, glanced at Mary Carolyn, yawned, and returned his gaze to the notebook.

Sebastian's eyes held a smoldering quality which he suddenly released in words. "Late!" he snapped, his voice vibrant with masculine power, "Late! Retarding my research."

She drew a deep breath and put up white fingers to hide the nervous tremor of her lips. But before she could even lower or raise her lashes appealingly Professor Sebastian's arm darted backward and in a second's paralysis of unbelief she saw him flick a small whip at her ankles. She jumped, crying, "Ouch! Don't" before it seemed possible she could have spoken. His face was stern, immobile. The whip licked her ankles again with a smart, stinging rebuff; she leaped upward with the pain of wounded vanity frozen on her face. The assistant regarded her with interest. She dropped her eyes and saw her feet hopping comically beneath the whip's compulsion. Her feet and her whole ensemble were so short of the romantic that they were ridiculous—Mary Carolyn would have died laughing if she could have seen them as a detached person.

She jumped again faster and faster as the whip stung her ankles into rebellion. The tears stood in her eyes. She was so furious with the sense of her ungraceful aspect that she could have shrieked. She pressed her lips tightly together, but she could not control her involuntary leaps when the small lash dared to touch her feet. It was not hard enough to hurt. it was the clear conception of her own ignominy that caused Mary Carolyn's eyes to blaze, her lips to parch, her face to flame with a furious, bitter red.

Just when she had been goaded to the brink of uncontrollable anger Professor Sebastian suddenly tossed the toy whip aside. He nodded to the assistant, who bustled forward and popped a thermometer under Mary Carolyn's tongue. At the same time Sebastian touched her wrist and took her pulse.

She glared at the two men while they exchanged smiles of satisfaction. They gloated.

"This is the best yet," said Sebastian. "Pulse very high, very high."

"Two degrees of fever," said the assistant triumphantly.

"I have never," said Mary Carolyn, "been so outraged in my life." She thrust the disarranged hair back from her hot forehead. She was still wretchedly aware of what appeared to be enormous red feet protruding from the clumsy folds of the draggled kimono.

Sebastian's voice was very soothing. "Of course, of course. But that is the purpose of this experiment—to determine some of the physical effects of anger. All the young ladies were furious. It was far more difficult to devise some way of angering the men. What did I tell you about woman's intellect being governed by emotion?"

As she did not answer but only stared at him with sultry eyes, he turned to the assistant. "Please enter these notes in the chart in my study." Then tactfully he turned to the window and looked out down upon the campus while she retreated hastily behind the screen.

VI.

When Mary Carolyn reappeared, after as careful grooming as her shaking fingers could achieve, Professor Sebastian moved toward her with a placating smile. "I hope you will forgive me. It was all in the interests of science you know."

She stopped short, noticing something so curious that she gave a little gasp. This intense interest in the research had made him sartorially unwary. Perhaps the recent physical exertion had caused the mischief. She acted on an impulse she could never clearly explain afterward—was it pique or revenge or sheer villainy? With a motion as swift as his own had been when he flashed the whip at her ankles, she reached up and tore the beard from his chin.

He cried in a voice that was almost like a groan, "Don't! Don't!" A contortion of wounded vanity crossed his face. "This is, this is unspeakable!" he sputtered furiously. His eyes glowered from a face that had grown darkly red.

"Why on earth," she demanded, "why on earth do you wear a *false* beard?"

He struggled to appear calm but his voice shook with resentment. "I—because I visit my mother in Chicago frequently and she would find me too impossible with a beard." He choked angrily. "However, I see no reason to explain my personal conduct."

She studied his face and found it unfamiliar and unprepossessing. It was no longer saturnine or romantic. It was young and indecisive and it had a very, very weak chin.

Mary Carolyn drew a deep breath. "Be sure," she said inexorably, "to take your temperature and your pulse and enter them on the chart. . . . All in the interests of science you know."

As she hurried out of the door she heard him calling after her, but she quickened her pace and went bounding down the stairs with excited, childish steps that belied her sophisticated clothes.

It was not until she was in the outer hall on the first floor that Mary Carolyn realized a most ridiculous fact: In her gloved hand she still clutched Professor Sebastian's beard!

She leaned against the wall and shook with laughter until she was limp and the tears stood on her cheek. That was why he had shouted after her so vehemently . . . and of course he didn't want to appear clean shaven in the corridors. But she wouldn't go back. It would be too ludicrous a scene. And both of them were still too angry.

"Emotion," she decided with a wave of relief, "has taken complete control of intellect. It's grand to forget intellect and be thoroughly mad at somebody."

She put the professor's absurd disguise in her purse and returned to the Pi Omega house. She found Brent waiting for her. With excitement still trembling in her voice she said. "Darling, I'd almost forgotten we were going somewhere for dinner. Do please forgive me, but I've had the most interesting time."

"What doing?" asked Brent. "The hockey game was swell. three to one."

"Psychology research." She made up her mind swiftly that she wouldn't tell him. At least not until next year when they were married and living in Chicago.

He looked unhappy. "You're really crazy about that stuff, aren't you?"

She stood on tiptoe and put her arms around his neck, pressing her face against his cheek—feeling how hard and strong it was, and still so cool from the crisp out-door air.

"Psychology is the bunk," said Mary Carolyn. She smothered fresh laughter just below the tip of his ear.

"I'm going to drop it. Fannicott will let me because I don't need the credits."

"Then you aren't going to teach it?"

"Nah," said Mary Carolyn, with disdain. "Nobody can teach it. You're born with it. It's an instinct, not a study." She began to shake with idiotic mirth, but Brent was wise. He asked no questions, he only kissed her hair.

A freshman appeared at the door.

"Oh, excuse me, Mary Carolyn. Telephone. Somebody's been calling you for the past fifteen minutes."

Mary Carolyn went into the boot and answered the loud, crackling voice of Professor Sebastian with gentle poise. . . . Then going upstairs to her room she reflected that it was a pity he was so distraught. She was sorry about his predicament. He was trapped in his laboratory, he couldn't leave without his beard.

She took her psychology textbook from the desk. Between two pages that described the symptoms of anger, Mary Carolyn inclosed the small saturnine beard of Professor Sebastian. She also inclosed a tattered romantic illusion, but she did not think about that.

After carefully wrapping and tying the book in a neat parcel, she clattered downstairs again to Brent.

"Darling," she told him, "I have to stop at University Hall to return this book to Professor Sebastian on our way to dinner. You won't mind waiting while I run up to his laboratory, will you?"

"Of course not," said Brent. . . . "Listen. Do you love me?"

"I love you," said Mary Carolyn, "and no psychology about it."

SEVEN

SEX AND THE SINGLE GIRL

THE U.S. ECONOMY had been floundering for well over three years when Mary Carolyn's story was published, but that young woman appears to have been little troubled by any of the ills that affected so many of her contemporaries. Undoubtedly, some of the magazine's readers were far less fortunate. They might, for example, have begun to read the March 1933 issue of the *Journal* while standing in one of the bank lines that formed before the new president, Franklin Delano Roosevelt, declared a four-day national "Bank Holiday" on March 5 to keep the bank industry from collapse. Indeed, if the timing described by Montross is taken literally, Mary Carolyn might well have been leading the junior prom (keeping the identity of Locke, Berkeley, or Hume in mind) in June 1932, when the "Bonus Marchers," an estimated 20,000 unemployed World War I veterans and their families assembled in Washington, D.C., to agitate for early payment of monies scheduled for disbursement in 1945.[1] Her own march into the Dean's office to demand a transfer back into Professor Sebastian's class probably took place sometime in Hoover's last month in office, when the numbers of unemployed reached over thirteen million.

Mary Carolyn may not have been cognizant of hard times, but the *Journal* surely was. Like the economy, it was reduced—from almost 200 pages an issue in 1923 to about 150 in 1933. Loring A. Schuler, the magazine's fourth editor, well appreciated the gravity of the nation's economic situation, although he was clearly not a Roosevelt supporter. More than one of his 1933 editorials fulminated against the initiatives of the new president as counterproductive. The effects of the Depression were also apparent in the magazine's fiction; several stories published that year centered on the experience of hard times and there were a number of pieces on how to make do with little.

In this context, Montross's heroine appeared as especially graced and privileged. As the saying goes, "She had it all." She was not only insulated from financial exigency, her creator endowed her with beauty, intelligence, and will to use both in the service of her ambition. "Pretty, clever" and almost a sure bet for Phi Beta Kappa, here was a woman who could choose any path she wanted. And since she had an extensive wardrobe, she also had the clothes with which to greet all eventualities.

What was her connection to spinsterhood? None—and that is precisely the point! There is a spinster in this tale, a woman who never actually makes an appearance—Miss Parmalee. Invoked twice by Montross, and characterized in both instances by the adjective "mediocre," she remains off-stage as a representative of a possible but unacceptable alternative to marriage for a woman such as Mary Carolyn. No, the "normal" college girl of 1933, no matter how talented, would not, could not contemplate following in Miss Parmalee's footsteps for long. The life of a spinster would not, could not, do for her.

Yet despite her normalcy and her advantages, Mary Carolyn came close to losing everything—her fiancé, her professional hopes, her dignity, and, perhaps, her chance at love and marriage. There most definitely was a serpent in her garden, but his masculinity turned out to be of far more dubious provenance than that of the original! This narrative, as is obvious, was permeated rather more by Freudian than biblically inspired references; instinctive drives and psychosexual "emotions"—perverse and otherwise—provide the source of the action in its plot; given that emphasis, it is not surprising that the author induced her main character to major in psychology. When Mary Carolyn, like Eve, turned away from what her creator deemed appropriate she was motivated at least as much by libidinal impulses as by her desire for knowledge. Too, her transfer of interest from her impending marriage to the field of psychology was hardly prompted by intellectual curiosity alone. Rather, her desire to become a "lady scholar" was clearly piqued more by the "extremely handsome" Professor Sebastian than by any clear intellectual or professional aims. In fact, she had fastened on a plan to pursue a career in psychology only "under the spell of his fascination."

Another "crush," the reader will recall, had also been important in motivating Helen Standish to reject marriage, but her love had drawn her away from heterosexual pursuits and toward a homosocial—or even homoerotic—community. In Mary Carolyn's case, however, desire for a man was the primary motivation for action. Indeed, she could not even begin to contemplate existence without such a relationship. Thus, her intention to prepare for a career could only be transient; it was inextricably linked to her obsession with Sebastian. Her fantasies had far more to do with strategies for winning his attention and love than with surmounting occupational hurdles and her professional aspirations are described as only one of a succession of foolish passions. Logically, then, the end of her ardent feelings for Sebastian also quenched her professional yearnings.

Heterosexual aims also provided the focus for the artistic renderings that accompanied the story. Where Rebekah had been depicted on her own and Miss Metcalf was shown only in the company of children or embracing Helen, the first illustration for this story featured a kiss in the moonlight. However, as the drawing suggests, Mary Carolyn was in a dependent position. As befitted a thoroughly well-adjusted young coed she was may have been romantically inclined, but, as was normal for a properly brought up young woman, she was also sexually inexperienced. Montross suggests that her lack of knowledge combined with her heterosexual instincts was a source of great danger; she was all too easily led astray by desire. With a slight, but knowing wink at the reader, Montross describes the young coed as so blinded to her own feelings that she can't even "think of the word" for her "preoccupation" with the charismatic Professor Sebastian. She is, the author indicates, so overwhelmingly obsessed with Sebastian that the mere memory of his "saturnine" features was sufficient to obscure her mental image of the man she was engaged to marry.

What is to become of a young woman who is so led astray by libido, so enmeshed in the toils of foolish and hopeless ardor that she is prepared to give up a prosaic but wholesomely normal man for an effete and affected snob. How is such a woman to be saved? Even repeated humiliation at the hands of her idol is not sufficient to bring her to reason; she is literally undressed by her passion. Only the bizarre whipping experiment in Sebastian's laboratory makes the abnormality of her infatuation—both for a professor who avoids beautiful women and for the field of psychology—clear. The danger of Mary Carolyn's situation is underlined by the fact that she is only saved through a lucky accident—the discovery that Sebastian's most masculine attribute, his beard, is false. That revelation, the unmasking of the object of her desire, lays bare the fundamental truth of his character as well as his face. He is a fraudulent male—a weakling with an "indecisive" chin whose "smiles of satisfaction" are directed at his male assistant and he is far too attached to his mother!

Her romantic illusion shattered, Mary Carolyn recovers her senses, rejects Sebastian and his ways, decides to "forget intellect," declares her trust in feminine intuition, and embraces her solid and forbearing fiancé. And Brent, that wholesome, athletic, and uncomplicated man who asks "no questions," responds only by kissing her hair. But, this story makes clear, Sebastian's beard is not the only falsification here. His romantic appearance—his presence as well as his look—led Mary Carolyn to believe that she could reconcile the demands of love and work. That may well constitute the ultimate delusion. The two are, this tale insists, quite incompatible.

Montross's portrayal of feminine options may have been a result of bitter experience—her own marriage fell apart in the very year of Mary Carolyn's debut.[2] But whether her motivation was personal or not, her position dovetailed exactly with that of the *Ladies' Home Journal,* which, as Jennifer Scanlon notes, through the 1920s and beyond consistently promulgated the view that "married women belonged at home."[3] Such insistent emphasis was clearly a response to a new reality—the *Journal's* focus on the perils (as opposed to the virtues) of working after marriage reflected a changing set of occupational circumstances. By the 1920s, married women (especially if they were well educated and remained childless) increasingly found ways to pursue careers that had been established before wedlock.[4] As one historian notes, between 1910 and 1930 the proportions of professional women who were married rose from 12 to 25 percent.[5] And "educated" women were more likely to maintain access to work after wedlock than were their less advantaged contemporaries.[6]

The magazine and its staff were well aware of this phenomenon, although they generally deplored it. A 1933 effort to name the "great woman leaders" of the United States, cosponsored by the magazine and reported in the very issue that brought Mary Carolyn to the public's attention, illuminates the dilemma that career women presented to the home-oriented *Journal*. Indicating that the public well appreciated female professionals, the twelve at the top of the list were almost exclusively social activists and professionals.[7] Of them, the editor said,

> Great women, all of these. Great leaders, with magnificent achievements to their credit—and some of them, still living, have opportunities for still further contributions to the welfare of mankind. They and the works they have fostered will illuminate a brilliant page in our country's history.

But the bulk of his comments were not, in fact, about this distinguished group. Rather, he took advantage of the occasion to deliver a rather unoriginal lecture on the virtues of what he presented as the worthier but less celebrated woman. "To this roll of honor," he said,

> there should be added one other woman. The old Greeks erected an altar to the Unknown God. The nations of the Great War have built magnificent monuments to the Unknown Soldier. And no memorial to the great women of American can be wholly complete without some tribute to the Unknown Woman.
>
> The wife and mother, she may have been, who in the pioneering days unflinchingly turned her face westward toward hardship and danger that the nation might expand.
>
> The woman who in every time of peril has sent her husband and her sons to fight for the preservation of national honor and integrity.
>
> The woman who has struggled, often against selfish odds, to make this country a fitter place for children to live; who has battled for better schools, for safer streets, for the elimination of child labor.
>
> The woman who has submerged her own self in the making of a happy, orderly home for her husband and her children.
>
> The woman who in the unhappy days of depression has valiantly carried on with courage, with cheerfulness and with confidence, in the future of America.

This Unknown Woman has no name—for her name is legion. She has no address—for she lives everywhere, in cities and towns and on a million farms, in great houses and small, in wealth and in poverty.

But without a public career, without honor or distinction, she is none the less the greatest of the great. History will not remember her, though she has made history. She will remain unsung in philosophy, though she is the greatest of philosophers. Scientists pay her little heed, though without her the achievements of science would fall on barren ground. And though she may never be recorded among the Newtons and the Einsteins, yet it must be admitted that a woman who has raised a family on a small income must be a mathematician of no mean ability.

And so, while we honor the twelve whose glory is so justly earned and blazoned forth, let us not forget to hail the thirteenth and to give her the respect and the acclaim that are her due.[8]

But Currie must also have been convinced that many women found his model of feminine excellence less than compelling, because in the very next issue, he issued the following lament:

There is no social problem of today that arouses so much bitterness of discussion and conflict of opinion as the question of whether a wife can satisfactorily combine a business career with the profession or function or whatever you may wish to call it of being a wife.

Nearly every case of the sort possesses its own peculiar psychology. More and more every year wives seem to be preferring jobs to homemaking, whether or not it is an economic necessity.[9]

Yet even as the magazine depicted the attempt to pursue a career after marriage as fraught with difficulty, it may also have unwittingly accepted the superiority of the very women it wished to criticize. A series of "sketches from the notebook of Faith Baldwin" published in the *Journal* during the course of the year are worth mentioning in this regard. They described the romantic and professional lives of four very accomplished women—a dress designer, the president of an advertising firm, a high-powered saleswoman, and a doctor. Each portrait integrated descriptions of worldly and romantic achievement—all four women had ardent suitors and three of the four eventually married. These stories (which may actually have been drawn from life) focused on the qualities that brought Baldwin's subjects to the top and the social cachet that attended their rise. Like her prewar predecessors, she emphasized the attractions of professional accomplishment. Baldwin's heroines had not only risen in status through their work, their improved class situation increased their attractiveness to men and, in consequence, enhanced their marriage prospects. But unlike earlier authors such as Margarita Gerry, Baldwin took the position that the heterosexual impulse was an essential characteristic of normal femininity. Her subjects not only found romance, they hoped and wished to marry. Only one of them would have taken issue with Mary Carolyn's briefly held opinion that it was possible to reconcile the "differing claims" of love and work.

Baldwin's tales, following the *Journal's* line, lingered on the price that women paid for attempting to satisfy both the appetite for romantic love and for a career. Inevitably, a conflict between the demands of vocation and matrimony undercut the ability of her heroines to follow the dictates of the heart and continue at the top in their professions. For example, the most successful of the women who figured in her stories, a high-powered advertising executive who believed most strongly in integrating love and work, was also the most deeply hurt by their conflicting requirements. Her success in the corporate world gave her entrée into elite circles. Courted by one of the city's most eligible and romantic bachelors and tired of living alone, she married her suitor. She did not think it necessary to give up her career and her husband knew better than to ask her to make the sacrifice. However, she found it desperately hard to live up to the incessant social demands of her husband's circle and accommodate the obligations of her job. Obliged to be "two people," she could not be fully successful as either. She became, says Baldwin "a tired business woman; a tired woman."[10]

The second, a fashion designer who had built her own establishment, was not so quick to marry. She too fell in love but, thinking carefully about her options, she reluctantly rejected her lover. As she put it, her work was so demanding that it left no time for anything else. Deciding that she was not "enough in love to give it up," she determined to eschew connubiality. Her lover was willing to wait however, and Baldwin opined that "some day . . . [she] will be completely happy if she can permit . . . [her business] a rival; or if she can make the delicate adjustment between the two."[11] The third woman, the doctor, was described as successful in merging the two, although that capacity only came after the death of her child and her husband's recovery from alcoholism. Only one of the women, a saleswoman who rose to be a "personal shopper" had no such compunctions; she happily threw up her job to follow her lover to his ranch in Montana.

Baldwin may have dwelt on the difficulties of combining career and marriage but she also made clear that women could sometimes manage to reconcile their conflicting demands. She said

> It's all a question of adjustment nowadays. It used to be simple in comparison. You adjusted yourself to marriage. Now you adjust yourself to marriage—and a career. Two differing claims.[12]

Doing both was clearly not easy, but was possible, she suggested.

> That, I suppose, is marriage—a partnership, and a growing to-gether, a burying of the past, a living in the present. Suffering enters in, and bitterness and rebellion. And regret; always regret. But such a marriage goes on growing, conquering.[13]

Rare though such marriages might be, Baldwin's pieces indicate that even as it deplored them, the magazine and its contributors recognized their advantages. In any case, at least in the *Journal*, spinsterhood was no longer evoked as a necessary prerequisite for women's careers.

Montross's story, which simultaneously accepted the possibility that a woman might seriously pursue a profession after marriage and rejected the idea as untenable was of a piece with a number of other *Journal* publications in this period. Brent does, after all, suggest that Mary Carolyn might try for an "assistant's job in psychology" after they marry and move to Chicago, although, he says, if she actually decides to train as a graduate psychologist, it would postpone their nuptials (perhaps forever).

The recognition of the vocational possibilities available to married women directly affected the image of the spinster. In the *Journal*, at least, she was invoked far less often than in the past. Miss Parmalee, for example, a woman who might once have claimed center stage in a college-girl's story, does not even make a personal appearance in this tale. She exists only as a reference point, one of those minor characters whose accomplishments were apparently so insignificant that she appears only as a representation of a representation. Based on this portrait and others that appeared in the *Journal* during the year, one might have predicted the spinster's imminent disappearance as a significant cultural image. Certainly her existence as exemplar of an alternate (and perhaps superior) form of womanhood was threatened. Taken as an omen of what was in store, the treatment of Miss Parmalee presaged a quiet and understated exit for her genus. Mary Carolyn, for one, regarded her so little, that she rejected the very idea of sitting in her classroom (and given the crowd in Professor Sebastian's class, her opinion was apparently shared by many other students at her unnamed university).

Alas, Mary Carolyn was hardly alone in her determination that spinsterhood was synonymous with the second-rate. Neither Montross nor her contemporaries regarded celibacy as an empowering alternative. Perhaps it was another of World War I's many casualties. Certainly in the war's aftermath women who did not marry (at least in the United States) were regarded with increasing suspicion. Barbara Simon, whose book recounts the lives of fifty such women born between 1884 and 1918 says that because Victorian and Edwardian notions of "respectable" womanhood assumed female sexual indifference, women who remained single may have "failed to marry, but they failed no sexual test." Thus it was that the white middle-class spinsters who were held up as examples of the best of their class (by prewar friends as well as enemies) came to represent one (although only one of many) of the postwar forms of psychic inadequacy.[14] So while the Miss Parmalees of this world continued to be assumed celibate and identified with professional aspiration, they were also perceived as sexual anomalies by the increasingly authoritative psychological establishment.

While Michael Mason has convincingly shown that Victorians were rather more "pro-sensual" than many suppose, it is nonetheless the case that Victorian and Edwardian notions of respectable womanhood assumed sexual indifference.[15] Historian Carolyn Dean explains that, for some time, "good" women were described as having little sexual drive and as being moved more by motherhood and spiritual union with a beloved than by erotic passion. However, Dean says, such notions crumbled in the context of changing attitudes toward sex and sexuality in this century and, as a result, heterosexual love was increasingly viewed as the "primary means of repairing selfdivision and effecting self-restoration in the alienating and fragmented modern world."[16]

Indeed, as many of the recent studies of the history of sexuality document, this century has witnessed an ongoing process of sexual revolution. In its earliest stages, the value, even necessity, of sexuality itself was asserted and, within a scientific generation, authorities from a variety of disciplines and practices increasingly accepted the importance of erotic satisfaction.[17] In the United States, that process was facilitated by the early and rapid acceptance of psychoanalytic and psychological theories in the popular realm.[18] Given the reputed capacity of psychologists to plumb the depths of motivation and Montross's apparent conviction that, for women at least, psychology is "an instinct, not a study," Mary Carolyn's area of concentration was hardly insignificant.

Theorists like Sigmund Freud and Havelock Ellis, along with activists like Victoria Woodhull and Rosa Luxemburg, had certainly promulgated the notion that sexual activity was part and parcel of normal adult life long before the war. The general acceptance and dissemination of these theories, however, were marked in the 1920s and 1930s by the proliferation of scientific tracts on the subject and by the assimilation into popular culture of their theories about erotic drives. The medical and psychological communities were key in disseminating a set of new definitions about the constituent elements of mental health and disease, including: (1) a legitimation of the "pleasurable and expressive qualities of sex,"[19] (2) concern about the negative consequences attending sexual repression, (3) the definition of sexual orientation as a category of identity, (4) a concomitant emphasis on heterosexuality as normal sexuality[20] and anything else as transgressive, and (5) the expectation that marriage (as opposed to motherhood) ought to be a central aim for the healthy woman.

Spinsterhood may have been defined by its supporters as an alternate path for womanhood, but in the interwar period it was increasingly associated with sexual pathology. Indeed, much of the psychological literature that appeared in the 1920s and 1930s is permeated by the sense that the generation that came of age after World War I had initiated a sexual revolution. So, for example, in the 1930s, doctor and Jungian analyst M. Esther Harding made reference to the "new attitude toward sexuality." "Doubtless," she said,

> in large sections of the country young people are as chaste as
> their parents—neither more nor less so. But there is unmistakable
> evidence that, in others, the old taboos have disappeared and
> young people, who a generation ago would without question

have been completely inexperienced in sexual matters, are now experimenting in this sphere of life. In many cases the incursions into the realm of love stop short at petting, but the number of young people who go on to complete sexual expression is very large.[21]

In this context, spinsterhood was increasingly seen as one of a number of abnormal conditions that suggested a lack of mental balance or a flight from femininity. If erotic impulses were "normal," the renunciation of sexuality was, in and of itself, a sign of pathology.

Given these changes in academic and popular perception, it was impossible to sustain claims that never-marrying women were the secular equivalent to nuns or were entitled to privileges unavailable to their married sisters. In a world that did not insist on the inevitability of erotic drive, the woman who abstained from sexuality might occupy a homologous niche—creating a gender possibility that undercut stark dualities sometimes associated with gender difference. But the claim that purity entitled unmarried women like Miss Parmalee access to realms that married women could not reach was, in the end, untenable. It was not only undermined by the emerging consensus among scientists of the mind and body that celibacy was a sign of psychological abnormality,[22] but by the increasing number of married women professionals.

Because the spinster's respectability as well as her social utility had been previously guaranteed by her (assumed) abstinence from sex as well as from marriage, this new emphasis was bound to be of some consequence for her sisters as well as herself. The spinster was able to operate as an independent woman precisely because she kept herself "free" of the concomitant engagements and obligations of "ordinary" women and her stature was measured by her distance from sexuality. The victory of theories that insisted on the inevitability of erotic drive inevitably destroyed those claims. As Leila Rupp notes, in the critical transition "from a world of privatized to a world of more public and commercialized sexuality" and to a gender-integrated public world

> young women . . . laid assertive new claims to their own sexuality, increasingly rigid definitions of heterosexuality and homosexuality cast more and more suspicion on a whole range of women's relationships. . . . women without men—whether 'spinsters' or

women in same sex couples—came more frequently to earn the label 'deviant.'[23]

Thus, while the spinster retained her status as icon in the popular imagination, the features of the admirable virgin of the century's beginning were retouched and her visage took on a less appealing aspect.

In this climate, spinster iconography changed dramatically. The glamorous, seductive figure of the early part of the century was replaced by a rather less powerful figure, one that was defined by sexual deficiency. However, despite that change in perception, the spinster remained a representative both of celibacy and of professional devotion—even if her achievements were undercut by her sexual incapacity.

As Sheila Jeffreys argues was the case in England, "the word spinster . . . was coming to mean, specifically, women who had not done sexual intercourse with men"; in the new as well as the old view the spinster was defined as much by her (presumed) celibacy as by her unmarried status.[24] The sexologists and their followers accepted the notion that respectable unmarried women were not sexually active even as they read permanent virginity as abnormal.[25]

Strangely enough, these assumptions persisted in the face of some evidence that women who failed to marry were not necessarily sexually inactive. A rather carefully conceived, although not representative, detailed statistical portrait of unmarried women appeared in a book written by Katharine Bement Davis in 1929. Of Davis's 1,200 unmarried, college-educated informants aged eighteen to forty-eight, approximately one in ten admitted to having had engaged in "intercourse" with a man and one in four had been involved in an "intense erotic relationship" with another woman.[26]

The issue of the sexuality of single women was addressed again in a book published in 1934. Issued as the second of a series by the "National Committee on Maternal Health, Inc." and drawn from a larger set of medical records collected by physicians (between 1890 and 1923), the book provides more evidence of authorial point of view than solid data.[27] On the one hand, the authors speculated that, for some women, remaining unmarried and committed to lifelong celibacy could be "a positive condition."[28] Accepting the notion that "[t]he strength of the sexual element in character prepares for aggressive manifestation of energy in other directions when sex has no direct expression," they found many examples of sexual energy redirected for socially useful purposes.

> Certain achievements of the single bring results. Frances Willard and Mary Lyon are hardly a lifetime away. Jane Addams is still with us. Florence Nightingale came to life again in Edith Cavell. Woman's colleges have single woman [*sic*] as presidents, deans and professors of distinction; students of the lower schools are formed in the likeness of single women teachers; leaders in religion, vocational guidance, recreation, advertising, business, social betterment, athletics, the arts and money making may be heard of every day. Without taking account of Feminism or of any artificial pressure, the examples of the conspicuous single influence every day the average single. Singleness seems possible because it incarnates achievement. The "inner emptiness, the complete inner freedom" which the church requires of the nun is here available for any chosen course.[29]

However, the authors also contended that energy might well be directed into less useful channels; remaining celibate was unproductive for some of the women in their records and was connected to neurosis or worse, insanity, although they were only able to look "incidentally" at these "other" means of "spending energy." "Seventeen out of the 350 women who were 'intensively studied' were described as "the most unhinged." Six were "confined in asylums" for some lengthy period of time and nine were "erratic, unreliable and manifestly alienated."[30] Of these women, the authors said:

> The typical patient is virgin. This is true both in limited anatomical sense and in the experience of love. Eleven have the hymen of anatomical virtue, four account for the admittance of two fingers by vaginal autoeroticism or pelvic examination or douche.[31]

In the mind of the educated and their followers, sexual inexperience continued to define "respectable" unmarried women and, whatever their actual engagements, the chastity of spinsters remained their most defining characteristics. A scholarly book written in 1976 by Margaret Adams, a self-defined "single," describes "the single woman" of the past; she *chose*, the author says, to remain unmarried and celibate and was devoted to her careers. Thus, spinsters furnished young women with models of good temper, energy and accomplishment, and devotion to others. Their celibacy was thus not only a career choice, it was also the source of their ability to do good.[32]

Only one of the American psychologists whom I found resisted that view. Jungian therapist M. Esther Harding, who, like Margaret Adams, never married and had also migrated to the United States as an adult, wrote a book in 1934 that directly addressed the issue of single women's sex lives. Perhaps, Harding opined, the cause of "the pioneers in the feminist movement" once demanded so much devotion that it replaced their need for "human love," but that was no longer the case.[33] She suggested that sexual impulses were likely to be as important for women who chose "work and an independent career, instead of marriage" as it is for those who chose to marry. Although such women were likely to repress those inclinations in the years when "their attention and energies were occupied with mastering a profession," she thought for some large number of single women such devotion could not last. Thus, while Harding agreed with the mainstream of the psychological and psychoanalytical establishment that sexual abstinence was required of women who aspired to a profession and that the resulting "years of unfulfilled instinct, long years of unbroken chastity" are a considerable "burden," she also opined that when such women reach their middle thirties, she said, and are

> free, as a rule, to turn to the emotional side of life . . . it is by no means uncommon for a woman of this type to fall in love. Her problem will be quite different from that of either the young girl or the married woman and her way of solving it, also, must be different from theirs.[34]

She maintained that there were four likely outcomes: repression, sexual attachment to an already married man, an affectional relation with another woman, or an explicitly sexual relation with another woman. And strikingly, as I understand her book, she actually saw the last alternative as offering the least psychologically troubling alternative.

Harding's view was shared by at least one other psychoanalyst, a woman doctor who worked at the Tavistock Clinic in London, Laura Hutton.[35] In fact, Hutton seems to have been so convinced that sexual activity was a prerequisite for emotional stability that she advocated homosexual activity as a useful outlet for single women and as preferable to nonmarital heterosexual erotic involvement.[36] Hutton described three types of spinsters: (1) a group that might be defined as organic spinsters, "women who, as a result of early emotional development—or rather arrest—are in any case likely to shrink, consciously or unconsciously, from the implications and responsibilities of marriage," (2) lesbians or, as she called them, "sexual inverted women" who "desire only another woman as a mate, who have no desire for marriage or for a man, but feel attracted, physically as well as emotionally, only toward members of their own sex," and (3) women who might be described as accidental spinsters, those who have been deprived (as a result of imbalance in the sex ratios) of what ought to have been their natural (married and heterosexual) destiny.[37] It was the latter group that concerned Hutton because, as she said, they had experienced a "barrier against normal fulfillment."[38] These women experienced emotional problems because they were sexually deprived, she said, but masturbation and what she refers to as masturbation "by another" could help to focus their energies.

But Harding and Hutton's explicit discussions of the sexual lives of single women appears to have been unique in a profession that was not generally given to reticence on such issues. While Freud suggested that the women analysts in his circle were likely to prove the best authorities on feminine mental life, none of them apparently took up the challenge with regard to women who were neither promiscuous nor wed. And one who looks to his followers searches in vain. The *Encyclopedia of Psychiatry, Psychology and Psychoanalysis*,[39] for example, has no listings for any related subject, and the three women who might have been expected to comment on such women in this period of time did not do so. Helene Deutsch, author of one of the standard Freudian texts on women's sexuality; Karen Horney, who was eventually read out of the circle for what some saw as her feminist attitudes; and Freud's daughter Anna, a towering analytic figure in her own right, were all silent on the matter. The latter omission is particularly intriguing since Anna Freud never married and lived with another woman, Dorothy Burlingame, for much of her adult life. Her reticence is somewhat startling since she seems to have been not at all loath to recount her own masturbatory fantasies to the world.

Contrary to what one might assume, therefore, there was little explicit discussion of any links between spinsterhood and homosexual activity.

M. Esther Harding (the Jungian) who did make the connection, was not very influential. Her books were not widely read; her theories neither entered the mainstream of the discipline nor found reflection in popular culture. So while both the spinster and lesbian were defined by the emerging "sciences" of psychology and psychoanalysis as "abnormal" women and while the never-marrying woman may have served, like the lesbian, to destabilize gender oppositions, the two were framed as distinct types. Asexuality was almost universally taken as a concomitant of spinsterhood; sexual activity defined her lesbian sister.

A new generation of scholars has shown that what seems to be "natural" is often dictated at least as much by culture as biology and that the "body" is constructed by art as well as by nature.[40] Gender thus has a history—one that has not, by necessity, been connected to biological realities. Drawing on the work of a number of anthropologists who have detailed the multiple possibilities for categorizing gender, Judith Butler argues that "one is not born female, one *becomes female*" because "there are . . . ways of culturally interpreting the sexed body, that are in no way restricted by the apparent duality of sex."[41] In consequence, she says today's "lesbian sometimes appears as a third gender . . . a category that radically problematizes both sex and gender as stable political categories of description." This discussion suggests that the spinster occupied a similar position in a previous age.

The details of the spinster's fall from grace describe more than her own decline in status; they had consequences for other women as well, facilitating and accompanying a narrowing of the understanding of "normal" femininity. That shift was made possible by an increasing emphasis on the importance of sexual expression for both men and women, a shift from a philosophy of "continence" to one encouraging "indulgence," and a new set of definitions that distinguished between normative and deviant sexualities.[42] This transition was a consequence of an increasing normalization of (hetero)sexuality both in the medical profession and within the community of feminists. The confluence of these tendencies not only undermined the representation of the spinster as an extra-domestic supporter of the family writ large, it rendered her dedication to career problematic.

Mary Jo Deegan makes reference to that transition in a recent account of the group of unmarried professional women whose lives centered on Hull House and the University of Chicago. She argues that in the period between 1890 and 1915, these women "were put on a pedestal and portrayed as saintly and celibate." In the ensuing years, however, they were first "mocked as ignorant, unsophisticated women who could not understand passion" and then increasingly derogated as "frustrated spinsters who sublimated their erotic drives."[43]

Yet while both the popular and scientific cultures felt less constrained about treating them and their work with disdain, spinsters did not, at least in those years, come in for the high levels of opprobrium that would attend them in later years. Rather, they seemed to fade, becoming lesser, often insignificant players in imaginative life and popular culture. In the 1933 *Journal*, for example, they appear only as occasional characters—sweet and somewhat helpless elderly ladies;[44] "a comfortable, clean-looking" nurse;[45] or a wealthy aunt who, opining that she is "enough of an old maid for the whole" family, helps her niece to marry the man she loves.

In conformity with psychoanalytic theory, women who remained unwed were portrayed as leading lives that were neither sexually nor occupationally normative. However, they were never threatening nor pitiful. Rather, they occupied a kind of intermediate although declining and distanced position in the theater of social life. Asexual figures, they remained somehow above/outside the fray of everyday life. In *The Women,* for example, a 1939 movie based on Clare Booth Luce's popular 1937 play of the same name, another unmarried woman, an author, makes a brief appearance. No men appear in either the play or the movie, and only this character, whose marginal position allows her an objective stance, is sufficiently free from the narcissism and competitive instincts of women who want to attract men to see the other characters clearly. Defining herself through ironic application of scientific terminology, she says, "I'm what nature abhors, an old maid, a frozen asset!" A writer and friend of the main character, her function in the movie, as in the play, is to provide trustworthy commentary on the womanliness of the heroine.

However, while the sexual revolution and married women's increased access to professional occupations served to push the spinster out of the limelight, they did not result in her vilification; that was accomplished decades later. Spinster iconography continued its decline during World War II as images of do-it-all women proliferated. After the war, however, the imagery reappeared, even though spinsterhood itself became questionable as a demographic reality in the wake of the attendant massive social, economic, and cultural transitions that followed the war. The sexual revolution, dramatic changes in nuclear family structure, and the beginnings of a revived women's movement altered the character and implications of single status for both men and women. Portraits of spinsterhood again proliferated, but to a new end. The never-marrying woman ceased to embody accomplishment; rather she came to represent a kind of statelessness; she became a pariah—a woman denied all that made (female) life worth living.

EIGHT

HOLLYWOOD STARS

IN ONE OF THE most revered of American films, *It's a Wonderful Life*, George Bailey, a good but despairing man, is given the chance to see what would have become of his community if he'd never been born.[1] Of his many terrifying encounters in the alternative, and Baileyless, town of Bedford Falls, one of the most striking is with his wife Mary. Encountering her as she walks alone on a darkened street, Bailey rushes to embrace her. But because he never existed, she never married and, consequently, she is not at all like his warm, loving, and beautiful wife. Quite the contrary, in the dystopic alterworld, she is a mousy librarian in clunky shoes and glasses. Walking alone through empty shadows, she avoids all human contact. Without doubt, she embodies the obverse of a "wonderful life."

Although the contrasting portraits of Mary Bailey are only one component of a larger allegory, for the purposes of this analysis they are absolutely central. The film was one of a succession of chilling portrayals of the figure that Marjorie Rosen once labeled "the woman alone."[2] Depicting spinsterhood as the "dreaded option," these portraits functioned to warn young women that, as Jackie Byars puts it, "if they didn't marry young, they might not marry at all." As such, Byars contends, they constituted effective deterrents to female participation in "new ideas and new social practices."[3]

Whatever its effect, however, given the spinster's past, this kind of portrayal reflected a new attitude. The spinster stories of the 1920s and 1930s seem far less negative. In fact, if the *Ladies' Home Journal* issues of 1923 and 1933 were good indicators of what was to come, one would have expected the immanent disappearance rather than the resurrection and vilification of the never-marrying woman. As exemplified by Miss Parmalee, the spinster had been so effectively sidelined in the 1933 *Journal* that, looking backwards, she seems to have been on the verge of cultural annihilation. And that is precisely the point; she was revived on her figurative deathbed. The spinster's return to the limelight during the war years is significant precisely because it was so inappropriate, given the character of the times.

Certainly the need to embody an alternate path for the achievement of (middle-class, white) female respectability had drastically diminished by the early 1940s. The exigencies of mobilization and combat definitively changed expectations of and for women, at least for the war's duration, silencing concerns about married women in the workforce and relegating attendant discussions of single professional women to the proverbial back burner. As America went back to work after the decade-long economic depression, fears that women were taking jobs away from men rapidly dissipated. And, after 1942, government agencies even mounted propaganda campaigns aimed at bringing more women into the workforce to meet existing production needs.[4] Working women were so normalized in these years that one of the heroines of the 1943 *Ladies' Home Journal*, a surgeon, dared to call off her engagement when she learned that her fiancé expected her to give up her profession for marriage. Her commitment to her vocation was rewarded in this story because she quickly found a new suitor: the head of her service, a man who encouraged her to be "a doctor as well as a woman," won her heart when, finding her drooping and tired after a particularly hard surgery, he told her, "I love the way you look."[5]

More, as a number of scholars have noted, women's workforce participation rates did not diminish significantly after the war ended. On the contrary, these were precisely the years when married women began moving into the paid labor force in substantial numbers.[6]

The demographic realities of the period also ought to have reduced the relevance of spinsters. Military losses certainly did not have a dampening effect on marriage rates in the United States; quite the contrary, the frequency of wedlock and the low ages at which men and women married during the war and after resulted in what demographers refer to as high rates of nuptuality. Indeed, as a number of researchers have noted, the members of the generation who grew up during the Depression and World War II and reached adulthood as the war ended were atypical rather than representative of "twentieth-century American family life." Ninety-five percent of women born between 1921 and 1940 would eventually be wed—more than any previous or later cohort.[7] In addition, they got married earlier, were more likely to have children, and had more children than any generation that came before or after. As William Chafe notes in his widely used text on postwar America, by 1945, there were "2.5 million fewer single women than in 1940," and by 1950 nearly 60 percent of the eighteen to twenty-four-year-old age group were married, in contrast to only 42 percent at the beginning of the war.[8] Even the *Journal* was struck by the statistics, noting in a 1953 "Making Marriage Work" column that "statistics show that today 89 per cent of all women have been married by the time they are 29."[9]

In addition to the decline of spinsterhood as a demographic reality in this period, the ongoing sexual revolution should also have undermined its cultural underpinnings. As the famous Kinsey studies demonstrated, during the first fifty years of the century, rates of female premarital sexual activity rose for each successive age cohort and, by the 1950s, teenage women were far less likely sexually inexperienced until marriage than their mothers had been.[10] That obviously must have rendered the possibility of permanent virginity far less tenable than it had seemed in the not-so-distant past.

According to one scholar, middle-class youth who "matured" in the late 1950s and after "not only accepted premarital coitus," they legitimated their sexual activity "by invoking discourses that were issuing forth from the very center of society."[11] Best-selling fiction and advice texts, mass circulation magazines, popular music, and art constructed sex as a sphere of pleasure and self-expression. In this context, the possibility that single women might be sexually active became increasingly obvious—so very clear, in fact, that the main aim of two postwar books written by Catholic priests was to reinforce the need for premarital chastity and to persuade unmarried women to refrain from sexual activity. "If," warned William Faherty, S.J., in 1964,

> the majority of single women in any society lost respect for chastity, the framework of sanctity around marriage would be doomed. Thus by her very renunciation of marriage and motherhood, the chaste single woman strengthens both.[12]

Given the spinster's fading reality and diminishing role, one might have expected that she would have become culturally irrelevant as well. Yet, paradoxically, despite the new demographic and sexual "realities" and a diminishing physical presence, the spinster experienced a period of rejuvenation beginning just after the economy had recovered from the Depression. It can be no accident that beginning in the early 1940s—during World War II—that repetitive references indicate that the never-marrying woman began, once again, to loom large in the American imagination.[13]

However, in these years, the attractive features that had once defined the independent (if latterly mediocre) unmarried professional woman—that female achiever of the past—were obliterated, and her visage took on a far more sinister aspect.

The transformation in spinster imagery is observable in the *Ladies' Home Journal.* References to unmarried virgins were at least as numerous in the 1943 as the 1933 *Journal*, but these wartime spinsters either had relatively unexciting and clearly low-paying jobs or were helplessly dependent. They worked as nurses, secretaries, dressmakers, clerks, or worse and depended on the care of others.[14] More, occasional asides indicate that the magazine's contributors would have concurred with Capra's 1946 portrait of the "other" Mary. In 1943, for example, one mention of the word "spinster" and two of "old maid" appeared, all referring to what might be described as the special vulnerabilities of women who remained unwed into what were considered the "middle" years. The woman given the title of "spinster" was harmless, but helpless. An elderly, foolish, and "childlike" woman, she was killed by her brother in the course of the tale. The two people described as "old maids"—a male surgeon who was afraid to undertake a delicate procedure and a young woman who was warned to drop her "high-and-mighty airs" or suffer the consequences by finding herself unloved and unmarried—were clearly more resourceful but far less attractive than their unfortunate contemporary.[15]

The growing importance of spinster imagery was apparent in other arenas as well. The psychological model, for example, was now applied to spinsterhood in a new way. Where the spinster of the Depression years was regarded as sexually "frozen," socially marginal and even, as in the case of Miss Parmalee, professionally and personally "mediocre," her successor was designated pathological. The now infamous, though often quoted duo, freelance writer Ferdinand Lundberg and psychiatrist Marynia Farnham, invoked her as a prime example of a woman gone wrong. In their influential 1947 best seller, *Modern Woman: The Lost Sex*, Lundberg and Farnham deployed the work of Helene Deutsch to advocate female domesticity. Arguing that despite the removal of "nearly every one of the earlier reasons for female anxiety," American women are "fearful and unsure" of themselves; they recommended a return to unqualified "acceptance and assertion" of the reproductive function.[16] Extending Deutsch's notion that the organization of female genitalia and the nature of parturition dictated a particular course for normal psychosexual development, they insisted that assertiveness, independence, and failure to bear children violated the basic premises of women's biological requirements. For them, all women who "voluntarily refrain from having children" deviated "from normal behavior." Spinsters, as a subgroup of such women, were particularly problematic, according to Lundberg and Farnham, because they were among those who, "renouncing" their "womanliness on the sexual level itself . . . could neither love nor inspire love."[17] Not only problematic to themselves, they were harmful to others as well.

Therefore, the writers suggested:

> All spinsters [should] be barred by law from having anything to do with the teaching of children on the ground of theoretical (usually real) emotional incompetence. All public-teaching posts now filled by women would be reserved not only for married women but for those with at least one child, with provision made for necessary exceptions.

Moreover, they were convinced that it would serve a larger societal purpose to make it difficult for spinsters to earn a decent livelihood. As they put it,

> What would happen to the spinsters? They would, perhaps, be encouraged to marry. If they did not, they would have to seek other jobs on the ground that they had not met the basic requirements for this particular, vital employment. A great many children have unquestionably been damaged psychologically by the spinster teacher who cannot be an adequate model of a complete woman either for boys or girls.[18]

An increase in the use of spinster iconography and a similar transformation in depictions of women who remained unmarried was also apparent in productions emanating from Hollywood. Indeed, a surprising number of films made under the studio system in this period included "old maid" characters. Some members of the sisterhood even got starring roles, especially in the melodramatic "tearjerkers" that were so successful with female audiences.[19] In these fantasies, where self-sacrifice was paramount, the never-marrying woman seems to have had a significant part to play in preserving American values and family life. However, in these fictions, her portrait had been so altered from former times that, aside from her lack of sexual experience, she resembled them not at all.

Spinsters had appeared in movies occasionally during the 1930s; as in the *Journal*, though, they seem to have had only walk-on parts. A short decade later, films began to make more use of them but the attention of movie studios was hardly a signal of new respect. To the contrary, along with some figures in the psychoanalytic establishment, Hollywood productions treated women who remained unmarried as extremely problematic. Like the alternate Mary Bailey, spinsters were almost always invoked to provide a negative foil for a preferred (female) self. For example, in the 1949 comedy, *Father Was a Fullback* the old maid was introduced as a metaphor for (female) hopelessness. In that movie, the teenage daughter of a college football coach (played by a young Natalie Wood making her first big-screen appearance) was so humiliated by her failure to attract a suitor that she despaired of ever marrying. Deciding that such a life would involve isolation, ugliness, and vicarious living, she rashly proceeded to give away her cosmetics, redecorate her room in a monastic style with a desk as its central feature, don an eyeshade to hide her face, and remove herself from all social intercourse.[20] For her, as for Capra, spinsterhood represented the opposite of the normal, the desirable, the good.

In the 1940s and 1950s, spinsters came to loom so large in the American imagination, in fact, that a few of them even got starring parts in Hollywood productions. Their stories must have been expected to appeal to a large audience because box-office favorites, Katherine Hepburn and Bette Davis, who both specialized in playing "unusual" women, took (or were assigned) such roles more than once. Of these *Now, Voyager*, starring Bette Davis and made during the war (in 1942), and *Summertime*, starring Katherine Hepburn and made over a decade later (in 1955), are of special interest. Despite the thirteen-year gap between the two films and their particular emphases, they nonetheless drew on similar views of women who remained unmarried into their "middle" years (then defined as the late twenties or early thirties).

The two movies drew large audiences. The stories were so memorable, the productions so engrossing, and Davis and Hepburn gave such compelling performances that they are now designated "classics." Indeed, *Now, Voyager* continues to engross critics, scholars, and movie fans to this day. Thus, these films are important not just because of their protagonists, but because they were "hits"; it is that combination that particularly commends them as worth discussing here.

Both describe a portion of the life of an unhappy and repressed woman who has previously given herself up (or been given up) to spinsterhood. But each of the protagonists is reborn, redeemed, and beautified through love. The tales were alike in another regard as well. They centered on journeys, ventures away from home, family, and everyday contacts into what Victor Turner has called "liminal" space,[21] where inhibitions diminish as the distance from the everyday increases. It is the voyage that provides the occasion for romance, seduction, and, in these films, a heterosexual outcome.

Like many movies of the time, *Now, Voyager* and *Summertime* were adaptations, the former of a novel and the latter of a play.[22] And while the films faithfully followed the plotlines of their originals, they also made key alterations in the details. The continuities and disjunctions between the filmic and original renderings are of particular interest here because they indicate what the filmmakers deemed credible and what they thought needed revision in order to sell the tale. Of course, films in general are useful as cultural informants, but box-office successes are especially worthwhile sources for information on American values at mid-century. Films are more likely to reflect common assumptions and concerns than the creations of the individual imagination because they represent the transformation of idiosyncratic creations into a collective idiom. Ironically, however, because the capacity to create images on screen that touch the feelings and imagination of the audience has proved rather more evanescent than producers would like, we can detect a fortuitous conjunction between the sentiments of the public and the contrivances of their makers in those films that draw the most viewers. So although it is possible to apprehend the constancies, trends, and changes in the "narratives of our culture" through an exploration of film practices,[23] those movies that are most successful in the mass market are probably the best sources of information about generally accepted and acceptable, often unselfconsciously asserted, social perceptions.[24]

Now, Voyager, Olive Prouty's complicated and (by current standards) overwritten 1941 novel, was turned into a no less convoluted and equally

melodramatic film in 1942. The tale centers on the transformation of Charlotte Vale, the unwanted daughter of a wealthy and prominent society woman,
who is almost destroyed by her cold and selfish mother. Charlotte has been
so isolated by her dreadful parent that "normal" feminine development is
impossible.[25] The result: unattractive, overweight, and unhappy, Charlotte has
a nervous breakdown.

Both the original and movie renderings describe the evolution of this
dowdy and much put-upon duckling into a swan. However, while the
movie evinces passion (both sexual and spiritual) as central to that development, the novel gives at least equal credit to psychoanalysis.

In the movie, as in the book, a cruise, a new persona, and a love affair
complete what Stanley Cavell describes as a "ponderously symbolized . . .
metamorphosis."[26] After hospitalization and psychoanalysis (an interlude that
is only briefly depicted in the movie) Charlotte takes the place and name
of another woman—Renee—on a cruise ship. Her appearance, improved by
her stay at the hospital, is further enhanced by the stylish new wardrobe that
hangs in her cabin—the seagoing appurtenances of her wealthy and presumably beautiful benefactress.

On board, she becomes acquainted and then friendly with another
passenger, Jerry Durrance (played by Paul Heinreid), an unhappily married
man who is traveling alone on business. To protect her actual identity (or
perhaps to confirm her new one), Durrance gives her a third name—
Camille. Then, their friendship is transformed into a passionate love affair
when, on a sightseeing trip, they are stranded overnight on a Brazilian
mountainside. It is a hopeless love, but one that completes her transformation, rendering her both beautiful and socially adept. When the ship docks,
she is so transformed that even her own niece doesn't recognize her.

The happiest of outcomes is not, however, within Charlotte's grasp.
Despite his protestations of eternal love, Jerry will not (or, perhaps because
of the conventions of the time, cannot) abandon wife and daughters. Yet,
even as she understands that she can neither marry nor go on seeing Jerry,
the knowledge that she is loved confers new capacities on Charlotte (who
now, though secretly, is also and forever Camille). After the cruise, Charlotte/
Renee/Camille finds the strength to resist her mother's demands and the
self-confidence to take her place in society. She is so successful in this regard
that she soon finds herself engaged to a wealthy and socially prominent
widower (a relationship that does not last when she realizes that it is inferior
to the one she has with Jerry).

Charlotte's story ends with redemption through self-sacrifice, as was often the case in melodrama. By her refusal to marry, Charlotte's independence is confirmed, even though she remains, alas, alone—an estate confirmed when her mother dies. Devastated by feelings of responsibility for her mother's death, she returns to the sanitarium for a visit. There, she encounters Jerry's daughter who, having been rejected as Charlotte was, has had a breakdown. Sympathy leads Charlotte to try to help the young and very uncooperative patient and then to foster the child, an act that reunites her (now in friendship and guardianship rather than sexually) with her former lover.

Faithfully following the outline created by the novelist, the film nonetheless diverged from its original through the placement of emphases. Prouty, for example, opened her story with a description of the protagonist after her beautification. Sitting on a sunny terrace, surrounded by freesias, as she waits for her "male companion" to finish a telephone call, Charlotte contemplates her altered self—the unfamiliar taste of cigarette smoke at the back of her throat, the entrancing appearance of her silk-clad leg and its modish shoe, and the feeling of her newly shorn hair at the nape of her neck.

The filmmaker, in contrast, introduces us to Charlotte before her transformation, beginning the movie with a scene in which her mother, her concerned sister-in-law Lisa, and Dr. Jacquith (a psychiatrist) discuss her mental condition. Lisa, who thinks that Charlotte is on the verge of a nervous breakdown, has brought the psychiatrist to visit over the objections of her mother-in-law.

Charlotte appears in Scene Two of the film, going to meet the visitors. The camera shows her hands hiding cigarettes in a drawer and then catches her again descending the stairs, introducing her to the viewer feet first (thick legs in ugly thick-heeled shoes), then full torso (the body of an aging woman, shapeless and ill dressed), and finally to her face (without makeup, framed by glasses, and hair drawn back in a bun). What is accomplished by transforming the bright colors that pervade the beginning of Olive Prouty's novel into the dark and drab images introduced in the movie version? While Prouty emphasizes the new sensual possibilities open to her heroine, placing a curtain of flowers between Charlotte and the coldness of her mother's home; in contrast the film begins by focusing on the ugliness and deprivations of spinsterhood.

Summertime, a steamy romance made a little over a decade later, features a simpler story line, but in some ways a more pitiable heroine. Like

Now, Voyager, this movie suggests that the path to wholeness is unconditional surrender to a man, even when he proves himself unsuitable or unavailable for marriage. However, the movie made some significant changes to the original—changes that were clearly designed to "universalize" the central figure. In particular, it reworked the characteristics and therefore, one presumes, the impact of its protagonist. To begin with (as seems to have been common practice at the time), the film eliminated the pronounced Jewishness of the spinster in Laurents's play, changing her name from Leona Samish to Jane Hudson. And while Miss Samish was very definitively rendered as a woman of the working class, Miss Hudson had all the accoutrements of social and financial security. Moreover, where the play made much of the family circumstances that led a working-class Jewish woman from New York to defer personal satisfaction, the film suggests that personal problems have deprived Miss Hudson of the chance at a normal life. Finally, while the people that both film and play heroine encounters are so engrossed in their own affairs that her isolation is emphasized, the play concentrates on her attempts to make friends while the film dwells on her sexual solitude.

Both movie and play begin as the unmarried protagonist arrives in Venice as part of a European tour. As she describes herself, she has come to Europe to find what she's been "missing all her life":

Something . . . [that was] way, way back in the back of her mind . . . a wonderful, mystical, magical miracle. . . .

However, except for the occasional company of a casually met street urchin, she remains alone and keenly aware of her isolation in a city full of couples. Tracking Jane Hudson's progress through Venice, the camera depicts her as overcome by the city. Filming so as to make stone into flesh, the movie portrays a woman bombarded by images of foreplay and copulation and reduced by buildings that are looming and phallic. In the play, Miss Samish is both single and socially inept because she has devoted herself to taking care of her family. In contrast, the Miss Hudson of the film is a bundle of inhibitions who, faced with the corporeality and carnality of Venice, shrinks from its very stones.

Both the waspy Jane Hudson and the Jewish Leona Samish encounter romance and seduction in the person of an attractive and romantic, but married, Signor Renato di Rossi, a philandering local shopkeeper. However, where the play emphasizes the cultural differences and distance between the heroine and her lover, in the movie version the Venetian lover (played by Rossano Brazzi), is an agent of transformation. In the play when the savvy urbanite discovers that her lover has not only hidden the fact that he is married, but that he is probably a crook as well, she becomes suspicious of his motives. Learning that she may well have been the victim of one of his money-making schemes, she breaks off the relationship only to regret her decision; her departure from Venice is, in consequence, accompanied by far more bitterness and regret than satisfaction.

In the film, in contrast, Signor di Rossi's attentions make Hudson a new woman. Divesting her of her pride, her camera, her sunglasses, and, of course, her virginity (the last accompanied by a display of fireworks), sex with him makes her prettier, more graceful, and even relaxed. Fulfilled, she is happy, even though she realizes that her affair cannot last and that she must leave Venice to preserve what she has. Boarding the train, she prepares for leave-taking in solitude. But her palpable sadness turns to joy when her lover appears just in time (and romantically) to wave good-bye as the train pulls out of the station. Like Charlotte Vale, she has been transformed by sexual passion, and she leaves Venice a satisfied, if still unattached, woman.

Movie romances of the period were resolved by marriage—the definitive ending to any love story. But these films were not comedies, they were melodramas, and their main characters were not likely to find unalloyed happiness. Consequently, the fact that neither Charlotte Vale nor Jane Hudson is portrayed as living happily (marriedly) ever after is not odd (given the genre). It is rather more peculiar, however, that Charlotte Vane and Jane Hudson are only saved (psychologically speaking) by adulterous relationships. Charlotte Vale is transformed into a beautiful and attractive woman and Miss Hudson is softened and fulfilled by a sexual encounter with a man who is already married.

This commonality, which reversed Hollywood's usual treatment of extra-marital sex as an immoral prelude to tragedy, is not only significant, it is striking because there was far less convergence in the originals. In Prouty's novel, the relation to Dr. Jacquith, the psychoanalyst, is at least as important in the transformation of Charlotte Vale as her love affair, and in Laurents's play, the affair itself leads only to a new form of unhappiness. Yet in the movie versions, the dramatic resolution requires both heroines to forgo, at least in each movie's time, the possibility of wedlock. Thus, the socially preferred conclusion to the romantic moment is prohibited by the previous domestic (even if loveless) engagements of the male leads. At the same time, "female desire," in and of itself, seems irrelevant to these films; the male protagonists are more important as catalysts for change as objects of physical craving. Indeed, Charlotte Vale and Jane Hudson are rescued as much by yielding both their virginity and their autonomy as by realizing any concrete aims of their own.

What does this accomplish? Both movie tales link spinsterhood to neurosis and mental illness, suggesting that it is far better for a woman to be unchaste than to be sexually repressed. The distorting effects of spinster-hood can only be removed through (heterosexual) intercourse. The two spinsters were crippled less by what they did than by what they had been unable to accomplish—that is, to enact heterosexuality.

Here, the contrast between the "woman alone" and the woman who has found love, however tenuous, is central. Presenting the opening situation of the main characters as abnormal and defining women through their need for men, these films outlined the characteristics of a "normal" female self and developed an implicit analysis of what it is that women, writ large, really do want and need.

In these and other movies (as had been the case in the *Ladies' Home Journal*), the never-marrying woman was universalized by her whiteness, native birth, and middle- or upper-class origins. But she shared another equally defining characteristic with spinsters of the past as well—her virginity. And like the spinsters of the past her lack of (hetero)sexual experience marked her as much as her single status. Neither the dramatic rise in pre-marital sexual activity nor the dissipation of the double standard had appar-ently led to any revision of that assumption. But unlike their rather more accomplished predecessors, the movie spinsters of the 1940s, 1950s, and 1960s were not privileged by their celibacy. On the contrary, it was this very characteristic that doomed them to unhappiness. Unlike the maiden hero-ines of the college-girl stories, Charlotte Vane and Jane Hudson were unable to marry because they were deprived of rather than rejecting a sexual outlet.

Once reestablished as a stock character, the "old maid" functioned as a recurring character in Hollywood films at least until the 1970s. Indeed, the spinster continued to linger on the set long after the sexual revolution had been accomplished—although more as a warning afterthought than as an inspiration. For example, the 1971 movie, *Plaza Suite*, based on Neil Simon's

1969 series of one-act plays, depicts a desperate father at the end of his rope because his daughter won't go to her own wedding. Having played along with several of his wife's failing strategies to move the expensive and delayed wedding ceremony back on course, he invokes a half-jesting, half-malevolent curse against his recalcitrant child: "Let her become a librarian with thick glasses and a pencil in her hair! Let her become the first spinster on the moon!"

In this as in other renderings, the central cinematic sign linking spinsterhood to isolation seems to have been the very object that was designed to increase visual acuity—glasses. Charlotte Vale's mother cuts her off from contemporaries in adolescence, for instance, by insisting that she wear spectacles and, conversely, Jacquith, Vale's doctor, signifies her readiness to lead a normal life when he breaks her glasses, saying, "You don't need these any more."

Patricia Mellencamp argues that the spectacle of the spectacle-wearing woman symbolized both knowledge and asexuality.[27] Certainly, in movies made during as well as after the war, the spinster's alienation from sexual activity was marked not only by a deprived emotional state but by enhanced vision. According to the logic of the day, the latter sustained the former. So, among other things, Charlotte Vale's cure involves learning how to dress well, to "go along with the crowd," and do without her glasses. Miss Hudson's eyes are also covered until love transforms her. *Summertime* begins with a shot of her in a train compartment. Already cut off from her surroundings, she distances herself further by gazing at the countryside through the lens of a motion picture camera. In the city, adding sunglasses to camera, she attempts to subject the city to her gaze and, likely because of her presumption, remains isolated and alone. The Venice that presents itself to her view is a city for lovers, one she can only observe.

With no apparent sense of irony, Hollywood pictured the female celibate as inhibited by the keenness of her vision; the very lenses that sharpened her sight also limited her access to "normal" life. In the opening scene of Alfred Hitchcock's 1941 movie, *Suspicion*, for example, an attractive young man (played by Cary Grant) is visibly repulsed by a woman wearing glasses. The camera follows his eyes as he examines the young woman who sits across from him in a train compartment. First he notices her solid shoes, stodgy suit, and the volume she is reading (it is, of course a psychoanalytic tract). As his perusal reaches her face, the light reflects off the spectacles she is wearing and he turns away disinterestedly. But glasses not only inhibited the romantic possibilities of single women, as Dorothy Parker's 1930's epigram about men's reluctance to make "passes" at women in eyeglasses suggests, they came to symbolize a flight from femininity. The unattractiveness of the Mary who has never met "her man" (in *It's a Wonderful Life*) is underscored not only by her dress, demeanor, and pallor but by her glasses—through which she peers in fright. Of course, the unmarried Mary is engaged in a reading profession, she is one of those accursed librarians!

Perhaps, at mid-century, attempts to block the male gaze could only be interpreted as disfiguring. Maybe in the context of male dominance, the woman who sees too clearly is unacceptable. Enhanced perception may have rendered women resistant to male privilege and thus immune to the heterosexual imperative. In any case, for Hollywood, glasses were not only deforming they were, in and of themselves, a sign of pathology. Earlier generations had seen glasses in a different light. An 1897 article describing the staff of the *Ladies' Home Journal*, for example, emphasized their happy effects. Of Louisa Knapp, the magazine's first editor, it said, her eyes "sparkle through gold-rimmed glasses." The same piece also credited Knapp's assistant, "Mrs. Emma Hewitt" (the author of Rebekah Spofford's Theory), with being able to see "a great deal of the practical side of life" through her specs.[28] In contrast, Charlotte Vale's mental imbalance is reinforced in the movie version of *Now, Voyager*, when viewers learn that her hobby is carving miniatures—an activity requiring great visual acuity as well as considerable talent.

Thus, the spinster who emerged in Hollywood during the war bore little resemblance to her predecessors. She was neither the fearless and accomplished standard-bearer of female independence of the early part of the century nor even the rather more marginalized representative of professional engagement of the interwar period. And while she continued to be defined by her lack of sexual experience, her virginity was treated more as a consequence than a cause of her situation. In these films, spinsterhood made women unattractive, rather than the reverse. Spinsters were unlovely precisely *because* they were unloved. The woman alone was depicted as excluded from almost all that made life worth living—she was defined and deformed through exile.

What are we to make of this imagery? It is peculiar because it was both backward looking and completely novel. On the one hand, it represented a cultural reversion, the revival of an old likeness that fit a rapidly declining number of living representatives. At the same time, the spinster of the 1940s bore little resemblance to her predecessors. They had been successful; she was a failure. They were professional and sometimes even glamorous; she was dowdy, even disfigured. Even when "mediocre," they were clearly competent to care for themselves; she, obviously, was not.

This iconography is intriguing because it could not have been Hollywood's creation alone; rather, it reflects an interaction between moviemakers and their public. As E. Ann Kaplan argues, the fact that Hollywood mothers were "rarely single and rarely combine[d] motherhood with work" was both reflective and constitutive.[29] Moreover, however male the cinematic establishment might have been, spinster portraiture cannot merely have been part of a male plot to keep women down. Men might have filmed Miss Vale and Miss Hudson, but they were intended to appeal to women; the movies could not have attracted large female audiences if their aims were to persuade women to surrender to male prerogative. Women, themselves, must have found the imagery meaningful.

In fact, Hollywood men were not the sole purveyors of spinster iconography. Negative imagery of spinsterhood was central to a "how to catch a man" book written by a woman for young women and published in 1963. The text of the book's second page (accompanied by a cartoon drawing of a woman lying on, surrounded by, and thinking about the letters "LOVE") bemoans the fact that

> [t]he modern girl, growing up in [a] . . . love-sodden atmosphere, is convinced she must love and be loved if she would marry with honor—a destructive credo which leads to many cases of spinsterhood.

Chapter two of the book opens with another reference to unmarried women, thus:

> ACTUALLY, if put to the test, few girls are so stubborn they would remain spinsters rather than pretend to love the man who asks them. The problem is—
>
> IT IS NOT SO EASY TO BE ASKED

Written in a lighthearted style, the book conveys a set of serious messages, including the following:

> it is, after all, better to be married to someone a little less than your ideal than not to be married at all.[30]

Clearly, derogation of spinsters like the "mediocre Miss Parmalee" at Mary Carolyn's college had only been a foretaste of what was to come! For the author of this book, heterosexuality, irrespective of desire, and marriage, rather than the mate, were the goals of normal women. Any deviation from that course could only be self-destructive.

Spinster imagery of the postwar period may have suggested that life without love was the punishment for women who couldn't or wouldn't knuckle under. But the lonely, loveless, and unlovely spinster was only half of the picture. The cultural landscape in which she appeared was balanced by another warning figure—the overbearing woman who was out to destroy the masculinity of her husband and sons and the femininity of her daughters. This threatening figure was repeatedly deployed in cultural productions of the period. Thus, in her analysis of *Life* magazine in the 1950s, Wendy Kozol says that *Life*'s representations of the American family, like other "characteristic" narratives"[31] of the day, repeatedly invoked the dangers of "weakened masculinity" and/or "overpowering maternality." Perhaps that is why Jerry Durrance and Signor di Rossi, who are both, after all, double-dealing adulterers, were rendered so sympathetically.

In this way films seem to have anticipated and followed what William O'Neill once described as a postwar retreat into domesticity—the phenomenon that Betty Friedan called "the feminine mystique."[32] The contrast between their portrayals of spinsterhood in the 1940s, 1950s, and 1960s and the images previously tendered by the popular media of the earlier period indicate a major shift in the cultural domain. It also confirms the contentions of scholars like Elaine Tyler May and Wini Breines that political and cultural concerns about gender reached new heights in the postwar period. As a result, young women were trapped between the imaginary scylla of the spinster and the charibdis of the destructive mother.

The transformation of the once powerful symbol of female independence into a feared and fearful exemplar was a central component of what now appears as a general attack on female assertiveness, an attack that permeates Hollywood productions of the period.[33] As Breines commented in what she referred to as her sociological memoir of the postwar epoch, the "old maid" stood as a warning against finding oneself a woman alone and excluded. Citing several studies that provide data on attitudes of the period, she argues that

> The fear, pity, and disdain for "old maids" were noteworthy. Repeated use of the term suggests its symbolic value in reinforcing

women's commitment to family. That "old maid" came up often in surveys about women's roles (and popular culture) suggests its centrality as a condition for women to avoid at all costs.[34]

Breines contends that this imagery was a constituent element of what historians now agree was a considerable postwar backlash against assertive women, connected to the politically conservative set of "containments" of the Cold War era that resulted in "relentless cultural pressure on middle-class women to become mothers and housewives."[35]

However, the timing of the spinster's revival and the negative spinster imagery that it occasioned suggest that those concerns were forged during the war rather than afterward, right in the midst of a successful campaign to bring more women into the workforce. The roots of postwar gender conservatism thus appear to have been planted in the very years when women received the most public encouragement for moving into jobs that had previously been reserved for men.

Resurrected as the media dredged the past for traditions that might assuage an ongoing sense of national crisis, the curious character of the spinster's reappearance underscores her significance as does the insistent quality of the stereotype. However, her actuality, the never-marrying, (hetero)sexually inexperienced woman, clearly had a significant part to play in the ongoing drama of gender concerns and possibilities. The axioms encoded in her portrait could not be proffered in sketches of married women—no matter how domineering.

Certainly, in these years, the sense that masculinity itself was at risk was fostered by a government propaganda machine that had been created to further popular investment in the war effort and appears to have been sustained both through the chilling winds of the Cold War and the hot reality of the Korean War. In this context, the spinster narratives produced by U.S. filmmakers both expressed a set of fears about and suggested penalties for women who sought to consult and satisfy their own desires.

Both *Now, Voyager* and *Summertime* were geared to a female audience and therefore their impact relied on the linkage between (female) viewer and (female) protagonist. This implied connection is especially important, given the degree to which loneliness—for women—is depicted as the central feature of life outside the family. In these films, only heterosexual engagement was sufficient for female completion. Maintaining that male affection makes women attractive and sexual passion guarantees them psychological stability had the effect of enjoining unconditional capitulation to a man as the price of love.

The spinster's new visage appears to have owed as much to concerns about endangered masculinity as to feminine ambition. How well that imagery functioned in sounding a warning against the potential consequences of female assertiveness or giving form to the fate in store for women who asked too much of men is not clear. There can be no doubt, however, that the negative spinster portrayals of the period served to define the "normal" woman more narrowly that had been the case half a century earlier.

NINE

AN IDEAL WOMAN

THE SPINSTER has been reborn several times in the American imagination. And despite her ill-favored appearance at the end of her life, for most of the twentieth century she was (marital status aside) socially above reproach. Perhaps for that reason, and despite recurrent attacks from a variety of experts, she received far better treatment than the other unmarried women who were also of interest to the mass media—the prostitute, the lesbian, and the unwed mother. Well-educated, white, Protestant, and, presumably, daughter of native-born parents, she was untouched by any of the disfigurations that marked other single women as socially unacceptable; so she often stood as the embodiment of the "other" acceptable life option for "woman" writ large.

Representing the only respectable alternative to marriage and motherhood, for many generations the spinster's lineaments depict what psychologists Hazel Markus and Paula Nurius depict as a "possible self."[1] As theorized by Markus and Nurius, individuals form personalized visions of what they "would like to become and what they are afraid of becoming." Embodiments of individually significant hopes, fears, and fantasies, they are "linked to the dynamic properties of the self-concept—to motivation, to distortion, and to change, both momentary and enduring." However, while possible selves are individualized, they are derived from "distinctly social" images. That is, both the best and worst conceivable selves are collectively created from a cultural repertoire—models, images, and symbols provided by the media—that can be tested against social experience. So, an individual's particular characteristics and experience may dictate which future possibilities are relevant or likely, but the pool of available types is culturally constructed.

The ubiquitous presence of the white, well-educated, and celibate woman as a staple of American popular fiction between the 1890s and the 1960s confirms her continuing viability as a "possible self," and testifies to her potency as a cultural icon. An adaptable signifier of female alternatives, she remained a constant element of what Janet Todd describes as the social unconscious.[2] Appearing in stories that were primarily directed to women, these portrayals encouraged the members of her audience to "try on" the image. That, more than anything else, may have been the secret of her longevity as a public figure.

I have argued that the spinster played a critical function in the long-running debates about women's nature, desires, and proper roles. But the changes in portraiture, and the corresponding transformation in what the image offered, suggest that there was a rather complicated correspondence between ideas about women who never married and developing concerns about gender, sexuality, and family life. Deployed, contested, and redefined through popular fiction, spinster imagery both delineated and responded to ideas about sex-linked possibilities. Therefore, the spinster was redrawn in accordance with the changing situation of women, but successive generations revised particular facets of her likeness without ever recognizing that a transformation was in progress. Perhaps for that reason, the fictional spinster was almost always invoked as a representative figure, even when her garments bore little resemblance to those of any conceivable flesh and blood counterparts.

In the late 1800s, when substantial numbers of women finally gained access to higher education and professional positions, the woman who remained unmarried and celibate was invoked as the very model of female accomplishment and independence. A symbol of female independence at the beginning of this century when marriage and career were considered incompatible choices for women, spinsters were celebrated by some and viewed as a threat to family life by others. Embarked on roads that rendered marriage difficult if not impossible, women who chose careers over marriage symbolized the epitome of worldly female accomplishment and therefore were proffered by more than one observer in answer to the much asked, and sometimes rather plaintive, query: "What do women want?" Respectable travelers on the alternate highway, in these years women who eschewed, or were denied, marriage were considered salient figures both by those who aimed at defending, and those who wanted to critique the institution of marriage. As a result, their garments were inevitably, though generally unconsciously, cut in contrast to the clothes of married contemporaries.

However, as career options for married women expanded after World War I, claims that the spinster represented a proxy, even superior, form of womanhood were unsustainable. In these years the never-marrying woman was increasingly marginalized as sexuality, or rather its repression, became her most defining characteristic. Moreover, even as the necessary association between female celibacy and career options dissipated, the idea persisted that the latter required the former. Once the spinster's celibacy, rather than her occupation, became her most salient characteristic, she was left with little in the way of cultural capital. Thus began her decline, and, by mid-century, she was invoked to model the characteristic features of prolonged sexual inexperience and inactivity.

By the 1930s the woman who had once been considered glamorous enough to seduce young women away from marriage was forgotten. The formerly fashionable and independent celibate now wore a considerably more dowdy ensemble. Despite all her hard-earned success, she was as likely to be depicted as an embodiment of mediocrity as a model of accomplishment. Although she was still deemed to be a socially useful creature, her limitations were reckoned far more obvious than her strengths and even when she was described as successful in worldly terms, she was nonetheless dismissed as limited by her situation. Sexually inactive, she was incomplete.

Perhaps fundamental to this shift in perception was the view that sexuality (expressed within marital relationships of course) was a concomitant of mental health for women. Here the perspective of the psychoanalytic community was important. Spinsterhood was increasingly depicted as a consequence of repression or a flight from femininity—in either case, a problem of psychosexual development. In consequence, although an earlier generation of spinsters may have been seen as selfishly abandoning family life, by the 1930s the unmarried woman was depicted as incapable of it. Portrayed as psychologically incapable of emotional attachment, her devotion to work was considered a sign of her mediocrity—the results of a failure in psychosexual development.

In this context, few continued to laud the benefits of never marrying. So, even though the image of the old maid persisted, the vision of self-sufficient and instrumental single-blessedness waned. According to the logic of the times, women could only be completed by marriage and women who remained unwed and celibate were necessarily repressed and incomplete. Because work was their only outlet, they were to be pitied more than scorned. Generally depicted as emotionally and sexually "frozen," they were also frequently rendered as rather more clear-sighted than their married sisters.

The glamour of celibacy was undermined by a new set of understandings of sexuality, but the never-marrying woman was not actually demonized until fears about masculine decline replaced race suicide and absent motherhood as a primary social concern. So, while much of the scholarly literature assumes that the rise of sexology was responsible for the derogation of women who remained unmarried, it was not until World War II that the most negative images of spinsters began to proliferate.

Indeed, although spinster images appear to have diminished in the 1930s, they gained new potency in the war years and after, even though the numbers of women who married increased, the average age at marriage decreased, and the numbers of single women who retained their virginity beyond the mid-twenties dwindled. The spinster's revival seems to have been linked to anxiety about masculine decline. As fears that women were usurping positions of power in the family multiplied in the 1940s, the woman who had once been portrayed as the exemplar of independent, talented, and self-sufficient womanhood was increasingly invoked as a symbol of loneliness and isolation. And the figure that previous generations had deemed so attractive that she seemed to menace the family's very future was transmuted into a young woman's nightmare.

These depictions suggested that women who were too assertive risked alienating potential mates and might well wind up exiled from family life. For that reason, invocations of spinsterhood became a kind of curse against women who took paths that led away from heterosexuality (and/or threatened men), even as fewer and fewer were actually choosing such a life path. As a result, despite, or perhaps more appropriately because of, a widespread concern about the decline of American manhood (and a concomitant emphasis on the high status of women in the United States), during the war and after there was little consciousness of gender inequality.

So, for example, few took notice when a new low point in the percentage of bachelor's and first professional degrees going to women was reached in the 1950s.[3]   Nor was there much concern about the 1966 figures indicating that the median wage of women who were employed full-time was less than 60 percent of the median wage of full-time male workers. As Claudia Goldin observes, despite dramatic increases in the proportions of women (especially married women) in the workforce, inequality was so naturalized it was rarely questioned, even by women themselves.[4]

In that context, images of the "old maid" could only serve to evoke powerful feelings of insecurity. However much young women may have aspired to worldly accomplishment, they could not have ignored the emotional consequences that were so visibly rendered in depictions of women like Charlotte Vane and Jane Hudson. Many women must have responded to the view that the only alternative to marriage was not an attractive option. Who would, in those circumstances, want to "go it alone"? Moreover, as work was no longer the prerogative of the unmarried woman and there remained no viable alternative to heterosexuality, there were few advantages to doing so.

Thus, the spinster's longevity was paid for by narrowing constructions of "normal" femininity as well as views about women who aspired to careers. If female adulthood required marriage, health and fulfillment could only be achieved through the love of a man. More, insofar as men were imperiled, so was that accomplishment.

Mid-century movie tales suggest that despite the dramatic alterations that were effected by time, circumstances, and design, concerns about masculine decline were accompanied by a dramatic resurgence in spinster imagery. But describing the reasons for the spinster's persistence completes only part of the puzzle. Unlike more enduring (and generally disreputable) female inhabitants of our culture's fancy, the spinster ultimately vanished from our cultural lexicon even if she remained on the scene for far longer than one might reasonably have expected. And that final piece of the mystery—the reasons for the spinster's demise—is the final subject of this book.

Of course, no one can say for certain, but I think the power of spinster imagery dissipated in the wake of mass insurgency. Beginning with the Civil Rights Movement in the mid-1950s in the United States, many Americans—most notably African Americans, Native Americans, a variety of ethnic groups, women, gays, and the disabled—began to reappraise political,

economic, and social arrangements. Organizing on the basis of identities that
participants had come to see as generally denigrated, grassroots groups and
organizations targeted forms, situations, and language in which systematic
although often unrecognized forms of inequality and discrimination pre-
vailed. Following and expanding on the protest models developed by the
early civil rights organizers, one after another of these groups sought to
make the often unacknowledged reality of discrimination visible and to
dismantle the structures that perpetuated and sustained inequality. In that
context, activists sought to overturn negative images and stereotypes as well
as to effect legal and political change. But identity issues were not only key
to mobilization, they provided the theoretical frame for action. Demands for
rendering the particulars of status and situation increased and conversely
attempts by the media to avoid representation of diversity became a cause
for further mobilization.

With the success of the new politics of identity the differences and
multiplicity in American society that had previously been ignored by the
mass media were made obvious. The old normative imagery fractured, the
differences among people in the United States became at least as palpable
as what they held in common. As a result, "universal" representations un-
marked by the defining characteristics of sex, gender, ethnicity, race, age, and
so forth became far less compelling. In this context, standard representations
of "the American woman" lost their cultural power and were far more likely
to be challenged than accepted.

Diminished by the increasing cultural irrelevance of universalized images, the spinster may well have been finished off by the very constituency
that she most affected—young women. And paradoxically the very power of
spinster iconography may ultimately have contributed to her demise.

Given the increasingly insistence on heterosexuality by mid-century,[5]
women could not conceive of a full life without a man. But if masculine
attachment to domesticity was increasingly viewed as tenuous and if male
dominance was taken for granted, men were logically in a position to dictate
terms, as women never had been. Therefore, women could not achieve
"normality" without surrendering to male prerogative. This was, I would
argue, a potent combination. Even as the resurrected spinster represented
failed femininity, she emphasized the existence of male privilege. There was
no choice! Or was there?

Mass culture operates neither in a wholly monolithic nor totally repressive fashion. As was the case in the college-girl stories in the *Ladies'*

Home Journal, cultural productions are "rife with contradictions, ambivalence, and competing voices." So, Joanne Meyerowitz demonstrates, while mass-circulation women's magazines of the postwar era rarely challenged essentialist views of women's nature or confronted the assumption that women had particular roles to play in family and community, they frequently "advocated both the domestic and the nondomestic sometimes in the same sentence."[6]

Indeed, while the spinster's image may have served a cautionary purpose, reinforcing conventional femininity and family life and delineating the penalties for subversion, it may also have provided some of the basis for growing discontent among women. The very fact that the alternate highway had vanished and that the accepted route to womanhood had become so fraught with pain may have intensified the sense of grievance and made a frame for insurgency possible. Moreover, the absence of legitimate models for independence and autonomy may have ensured that any tendency to struggle against the confines of "normal" femininity would require rebellious action. For these reasons, while spinster iconography of the period may have warned young women about the consequences of refusing to give in to men, it may also have created the opportunity to contemplate new possibilities for life outside the traditional family.

So even though the image of the "old maid" clearly functioned to limit the aspirations of many young women in the short term—especially those who were white, economically privileged, and academically precocious—in the long term it may have had rather different effects. It may have created the elements of a contentious stance that negated the warning. After all, the very same women whose recollections of the repressive consequences of spinster imagery were described in the first chapter of this book became feminists as well as scholars. And while they may well have feared winding up alone, they recount those concerns today as part of a feminist apologia.

How ironic! The woman who had been the repository of so many of the aspirations of the "first wave" of twentieth-century feminists may well have been done in by the shock troops of the "second wave"—those assertive young women who came of age in the late 1960s and 1970s and became the activist center of the women's liberation movement. Certainly, the spinster seems to have disappeared in the context of the gender revolution that they initiated.

As women's claims to equality bore fruit and their capacity to live independently of men increased, their marital status (or lack of it) became increasingly irrelevant. Moreover, as women continued to enter the workforce in larger and larger numbers, and families without men became more common, threatening women with exile from domestic life was hardly much of a deterrent to female assertiveness. Indeed, the dramatic increase in the diversity of family types and a concomitant rise in the numbers of self-supporting single mothers have today rendered women and their children the irreducible and central elements of family life.[7]

But the victory has hardly been complete. The single mother is more often viewed as a social problem than a social solution and she is rarely held up as a mirror for feminine aspiration. Today, as in the past, men and masculinity are viewed as the ultimate victims of an ongoing gender crisis, but the reasons for unease have changed.

During the early part of the century most commentators assumed that men benefited far more than the "gentler" sex from domestic arrangements. Thus, the fear arose that, given the option, young women would quite gladly avoid the toils of married life, the need to make do, and the concomitant obligation to find new ways of cooking cabbage. Indeed, as the stories reprinted here suggest, most observers were convinced that marriage was so difficult that only the desire for children and the rewards of motherhood were strong enough to dim the light that beckoned so seductively. In those days, women seemed far more likely than men to abandon hearth and home.

Today, however, concerns about men leaving the family have replaced earlier worries about the immanent departure of women. In the years that followed the Great Depression and World War II, men were described as having become dangerously impervious to domestic obligations.[8] Certainly, by the 1960s, Barbara Ehrenreich contends, cultural productions depicted men as natural bachelors, only loosely tied to the responsibilities that awaited any male who undertook obligations of husband.[9] And public concern does seem to have shifted from the menace posed by independent women to concern about the detachment of men from their families. As sociologist Judith Stacey recently said, "The premise that the growing incidence of fatherlessness is a social calamity" is so widely accepted that no scholarship seems able to undermine it.[10]

As this investigation of spinster portraiture has made clear, concerns about spinsters (and the single women who are their successors) have always been connected to worries about family life. Those who colored in the features of those respectable, but sexually inexperienced women were also responding to, as well as participating in the creation of, a set of understandings about the gendered origins of threats to the family. The persistence of the unmarried celibate in the face of widely accepted claims about the universality of the (hetero)sexual instinct and the consequences of repression indicates that the resilience of spinster imagery matched its malleability.

At the same time, ideas about spinsterhood both produced and responded to real practice. As Dorothy Smith said in a discussion of women's fashions, women create themselves at least partially in the context of "a textually-mediated discourse" on femininity, a " 'conversation', conducted through the written word, among speakers and hearers separated from one another in time and space." Femininity, Smith argued, has not only been a discursive project from the outset, it has been vested in the texts of mass and popular culture such as women's magazines, films, and, in recent years, television. However, while such discourse connects the marketing of products to what women do and to the "norms and images regulating the presentation of selves in social circles," the text neither dictates meaning nor has "overriding power." Not everything that a text says is in the text. It is the specific context that provides the interpretive index for understanding and implementation and, simultaneously, "local effects . . . arise from the textual ubiquity coding femininity and structuring relationships in various settings of the everyday world."[11]

Because of her respectable (if not consistently respected) status, the spinster continued to hold a unique position in the national imagination at least into the sixth decade of this century. Indeed, as this book has attempted to show, she became such a central, if unacknowledged, symbol of alternate potential that her cultural value persisted long after her demographic decline. She remained significant so long as discussions about the nature and possibilities of "normal" femininity persisted. Much has been made, in recent years, of the tendency to define the self and the characteristics of normalcy through the creation of categories of persons who are "other." This book has tried to avoid the kind of linguistic morass that sometimes surrounds such discussions, yet it should by now have become clear that the material in this book makes direct use of that theoretical perspective. As we have seen, the spinster's "otherness" both defined the normal and undermined it.

Today, when experts talk about single women as a "problem," they are likely referring to women who have children rather than to celibates. Now, as in the past, some women live their lives without marrying; like yesterday's "old maids" they stand as exemplars of an alternative. But they are never called spinsters and bear no resemblance to the celibate, childless, and professionally oriented figures that were so much a part of our cultural past. Quite the contrary, they stand as objects of public concern, precisely because of their sexual activity and their reproductive success. Thus, while it is certainly possible to discern some of the elements that defined spinsterhood in "the liberated woman," "the career woman, "the lesbian," the "single woman," or the "unmarried woman," no one of these figures occupies a similar niche in the social imagination. Still, although the spinster may have disappeared, we continue to grapple with concerns about women's desires and "the future of the family."

NOTES

CHAPTER ONE

1. This designation appeared in a book by Laurence James McCauley who identified himself as a priest and therapist. It was entitled *The Single Woman* (New York: Duell, Sloan & Pearce, 1952).

2. Arthur Conan Doyle, "The Silver Blaze" [originally published in *Strand Magazine*, 1892] *Adventures of Sherlock Holmes*, ed. by Edgar W. Smith (New York: The Heritage Press, 1950), pp. 515–539.

3. Information on marital status was found for 186 out of 202 women. Of this number, 53, or 25 percent of the total number, and 28 percent of those for whom we had marital status information remained single. For further information on the group, see Naomi Rosenthal et al., "Social Movements and Network Analysis: A Case Study of Nineteenth Century Women's Reform in New York State, *American Journal of Sociology* (90:5, 1985), pp. 1022–1054.

4. Linda Gordon, *Woman's Body, Woman's Rights* (New York: Penguin Books, 1977), p. 480.

5. Nancy Peterson, *Our Lives for Ourselves: Women Who Have Never Married* (New York: Putnam's Sons, 1981), p. 15.

6. A radical lesbian magazine has been entitled *Spinster*, for example. For other examples of reclaiming, see also the introductory essays in Laura Doan, ed., *Old Maids to Radical Spinsters: Unmarried Women in the Twentieth-Century Novel* (Urbana: University of Illinois Press, 1991) and Sheila Jeffreys' book, *The Spinster and Her Enemies* (London: Pandora Press, 1985).

7. *Story of a Pioneer*, with Elizabeth Jordan (New York: Harper and Bros., 1915). Shaw was born in 1847 and lived into her seventies.

8. Such a communal loss of memory, sidestepping or ignoring elements of the past that are likely to prove uncomfortable to keep in mind, has been labeled "social amnesia" by Russell Jacoby in *Social Amnesia: A Critique of Contemporary Psychology from Adler to Laing* (Boston: Beacon Press, 1975), pp. 3–4.

9. *Pocahontas: The Evolution of an American Narrative* (New York: Cambridge University Press, 1994), p. 1

10. *Frame Analysis* (New York: Harper, 1974), pp. 10–13.

11. *The Incorporation of America: Culture and Society in the Gilded Age* (New York: Hill and Wang, 1982), p. 8.

12. Helen Damon-Moore, *Magazines for the Millions: Gender and Commerce in the Ladies' Home Journal and the Saturday Evening Post, 1880–1910* (Albany: SUNY Press, 1994), chapter 1.

13. Ibid., p. 26.

14. New York: Harper & Bros., 1947.

15. Translated by Stella Browne (New York: Random House, 1930).

16. Dawn H. Currie, "Decoding Femininity: Advertisements and Their Teenage Readers," *Gender and Society* (11:4, 1997), pp. 460–461.

17. "Feminist Desire and Feminist Pleasure: On Janice Radway's *Reading the Romance: Women, Patriarchy and Popular Literature. Camera Obscura* (v. 16, 1988), pp. 134–176.

18. Dorothy Smith, "Femininity as Discourse," in *Becoming Feminine: The Politics of Popular Culture,* ed. by L. Roman and L. K. Christian-Smith (Philadelphia: Falmer, 1988), pp. 37–59.

19. C. T. Onions, *Shorter Oxford English Dictionary on Historical Principles* (Oxford: Oxford University Press, 1939).

20. Ibid.

21. There is now a substantial body of work on representation of spinsters in Victorian literature. However, most of that work has focused on the English context. I would argue, however, that while a common language and literature inevitably meant that there was considerable exchange of cultural production across the Atlantic, and although there was considerable overlap in ideas about women, there was also sufficient difference between the two countries to warrant a divergence in the histories of the idea of spinsterhood.

22. In "The Dating of the American Sexual Revolution: Evidence and Interpretation," in *The American Family in Social-Historical Perspective,* 2nd ed., ed. by Michael Gordon (New York: St. Martin's Press, 1978), Daniel Scott Smith summarizes the results of a study of premarital pregnancy. His study of premarital pregnancy rates was based on a sampling of records, largely confined to the New England region. His findings indicated fairly high premarital pregnancy rates for both the eighteenth and nineteenth century as follows:

PERIOD	PERCENT OF FIRST BIRTHS WITHIN NINE MONTHS OF MARRIAGE
Before 1701	11%
1701–1760	23%
1761–1800	34%
1801–1840	25%
1841–1880	16%

Of course, Smith's data included only women who eventually married; conclusions about the sexual experience of women who never married cannot be drawn from these figures. However, Smith's data clearly indicate that some substantial percentage of young women did engage in coitus while they were single and that a presumption of chastity, based on marital status alone, was unwarranted.

23. For a lengthy discussions about this issue, see especially Lilian Faderman's *Surpassing the Love of Men* (New York: Morrow, 1981) and Michael Mason, *The Making of Victorian Sexuality* (Oxford: Oxford University Press, 1995).

24. In his seminal article, "Family Limitation, Sexual Control, and Domestic Feminism in Victorian America," *A Heritage of Her Own: Toward a New Social History of American Women*, ed. by Nancy F. Cott and Elizabeth Pleck (New York: Simon and Shuster, 1979), Daniel Scott Smith cites the rates of 11 percent for the cohort born between 1865 and 1869 as the highest in American history.

25. Mary Jo Bane, *Here to Stay* (New York: Basic Books, 1976), p. 22, and Carl N. Degler, *At Odds: Women and the Family in American from the Revolution to the Present* (Oxford: Oxford University Press), 1980, p. 152.

26. Elaine Tyler May, *Barren in the Promised Land: Childless Americans and the Pursuit of Happiness* (New York: Basic Books, 1995), p. 50.

27. Lee Chambers-Schiller, *Liberty A Better Husband: Single Women in America: The Generations of 1780–1840* (New Haven: Yale University Press, 1984), chapter 1.

28. These stories turned up through a sampling process. I read all issues of the *Journal* for selected years as follows: 1884, 1888, 1890, 1893, and every tenth year afterward. In my sampling of material from 1884–86 and 1888–89, I looked only at four years out of the first ten (1884, 1885, 1889, 1890, and 1893) and therefore it is possible that the college "girl" did make her first appearance somewhat earlier. However, because I sampled more years in the magazine's first decade than in successive periods, and since at least one article on college women appeared in every volume I looked at after 1890, I can say with some confidence that she appeared as a magazine regular after that date.

29. Barbara Solomon reports that the average age of Radcliffe graduates between 1890 and 1900, for example, was twenty-nine. She thinks that this figure was typical for woman in the college population rather than anomalous. *In the Company of Educated Women* (New Haven: Yale University Press, 1985), chapter 8, p. 70.

30. Ibid., p. 62. Solomon's figures indicate that only 2.2 percent of women aged 18–21 went to college in 1890. By 1930, the proportion had risen to approximately 1 in 10. Even so, women constituted 36 percent of all college students in 1890 and 44 percent in 1930.

31. Such coverage ended, however, after the *Journal* narrowed its target audience after World War II and its contents were more narrowly directed at homemakers.

32. That determination is especially interesting given the fact that all the authors of the tales—Emma Hewitt (b. 1850), Margarita Spalding Gerry (b. 1870), and Lois Montross (b. 1897)—had been married.

33. Jennifer Scanlon, *Inarticulate Longings: The Ladies' Home Journal, Gender, and the Promise of Consumer Culture* (New York: Routledge, 1994), p. 62.

34. Graeme Turner, *Film as Social Practice* (London: Routledge, 1993), p. 70.

35. Elizabeth Cowie, *Representing the Woman: Cinema and Psychoanalysis* (Minneapolis: University of Minnesota Press, 1997), p. 303.

36. "Woman as Genre" in Janet Todd, *Women and Film* (New York: Holmes and Meier, 1988), pp. 130–42.

37. One of the early products of the women's studies movement in higher education was Marjorie Rosen's *Popcorn Venus* (New York: Coward McCann & Geoghan, 1973), a discussion of the image of women in the movies. For recent and more sophisticated and nuanced treatment, see Janet Todd, *Women and Film* and Patricia Ehrens, *Issues in Feminist Film Criticism* (Bloomington: Indiana University Press, 1990).

CHAPTER TWO

1. *Ladies' Home Journal* (hereafter *LHJ*), September 1890, pp. 3–4.

2. According to Helen Damon-Moore, Hewitt served as the *Journal's* associate editor for fifteen years. *Magazines for the Millions* (New York: State University of New York Press, 1994), p. 30.

CHAPTER THREE

1. Jennifer Scanlon argues that the *Journal* and other women's magazines of the period "obscured fundamental differences among women in every issue." They did so, she claims, by creating the "average"—a white, middle-class, native-born woman who was "truly modern" in both her style of life and her consumption patterns. Although this figure "left out as many women as she included, Scanlon points out, she "increasingly came to define womanhood for the early twentieth century" and "her limitations would form the composite of women's possibilities." *Inarticulate Longings: The Ladies Home Journal, Gender, and the Promises of Consumer Culture* (New York and London: Routledge, 1995), pp. 6–7.

2. See especially Claudia Goldin, *Understanding the Gender Gap: An Economic History of American Women* (New York: Oxford University Press, 1990), chapter 2.

3. But as legal historian Joan Hoff points out, "Most state legislators voted for the Married Women's Property Acts on the basis of conservative economic reasoning designed to protect, not to liberate, women." *Law, Gender & Injustice: A Legal History of U.S. Women* (New York: New York University Press, 1991), p. 128.

4. This event is described in Eleanor Flexner's book *Century of Struggle: The Woman's Rights Movement in the United States* (Cambridge: Harvard University Press, rev. ed. 1975), p. 75.

5. See especially Nancy Cott's book *The Bonds of Womanhood: Woman's Sphere" in New England, 1780–1835* (New Haven: Yale University Press, 1977) and Carrol Smith-Rosenberg's, *Disorderly Conduct: Visions of Gender in Victorian America* (New York: Oxford University Press, 1985).

6. For a discussion of the perception of this "new" woman in the popular press in the United States and Britain, see Patricia Marks, *Bicycles, Bangs, and Bloomers: The New Woman in the Popular Press* (Lexington: The University Press of Kentucky, 1990).

7. Margery Davies, *Woman's Place Is at the Typewriter: Office Work and Office Workers 1870–1930* (Philadelphia: Temple University Press, 1982).

8. Ann Swidler, "Culture in Action: Symbols and Strategies," *American Journal of Sociology*, 51:2 (1986), p. 273.

9. Laura Bohannon, "Shakespeare in the Bush" in *Anthropology for the Eighties*, ed. by Johnetta B. Cole (New York: Free Press, 1982). In this classic article, Bohannon says that when she was called on to contribute a story to the quotidian issue, she chose to tell one of the tales that many, in the West, consider a "universal" tale. She notes, with some amusement, that the story of Hamlet was well appreciated by her attentive audience, but for unexpected reasons. Her African friends, for example, murmured approvingly on learning of Claudius's marriage to his brother's wife.

10. Conversely, of course, a work such as *Walden*, written by Henry Thoreau and published in 1854, did not find an appreciative audience until some years after the death of its creator.

11. James Lynn, "Introduction" in *Women and Film*, ed. by Janet Todd (New York: Holmes and Meier, 1988), pp. 3–4.

12. Igor Kopytoff, "Women's Roles and Existential Identities," in *Beyond the Second Sex*, ed. by Peggy Sanday and Ruth Goodenough (College Park: University of Pennsylvania Press, 1990).

13. Barbara Solomon, *In the Company of Educated Women: A History of Women & Higher Education in America* (New Haven: Yale University Press, 1985).

14. John De'Emilio and Estelle B. Freedman, *Intimate Matters* (New York: Harper and Row, 1988), p. 190.

15. In addition, however, my colleague, Amanda Frisken, who has made an intensive study of cartoons of the period, says that lack of physical description in both prose and illustrations, intensifies what she describes as Rebekah's "curious" asexuality.

16. She signed at least one *Journal* column ("Scribbler's Letter to Gustavus" No. 2, September 1885, p. 6) as Mrs. Emma C. Hewitt.

17. "Homes of Single Women," in *Elizabeth Cady Stanton, Susan B. Anthony: Correspondence, Writings, Speeches*, ed. by Ellen DuBois (New York: Schocken Books, 1981), pp. 146–151.

18. "Modern Sexuality and the Myth of Victorian Repression," in *Passion and Power: Sexuality in History*, ed. by Kathy Peiss and Christina Simmons (Philadelpia: Temple University Press, 1989), p. 159.

19. "Passionlessness: An Interpretation of Victorian Sexual Ideology, 1790–1850," in *Signs: Journal of Women in Culture and Society* (4:2, 1978), p. 236.

20. Founded in late 1883 by editor Louisa Knapp Curtis and her spouse, publisher Cyrus Curtis, from its earliest issues, the editors hoped to capture a mass audience and geared the magazine's content to that end. In this, the publisher and editor were successful beyond any initial expectations. Boasting an astonishing fourfold growth during the magazine's second year (from 25,000 to 100,000 subscribers), in November 1885 Knapp's editorial described "the object of our present desire" as doubling readership again, presumably in an equally short period of time (*LHJ*, Editorial Notes, p. 4). And she was not far amiss in her projections. In 1888, the publisher counted "half a million permanent, yearly subscribers" who "have unbounded faith and confidence in every line we publish" as responsible for making the *Journal* "the leading advertising medium of the country."

21. Helen Damon-Moore, *Magazines for the Millions: Gender and Commerce in the Ladies' Home Journal and the Saturday Evening Post 1880–1910* (Albany: State University of New York Press, 1994) and Jennifer Scanlon, *Inarticulate Longings.*

22. Helen Damon-Moore, *Magazines for the Millions*, p. 37.

23. Jennifer Scanlon, *Inarticulate Longings*, p. 2.

24. Mrs. Emma C. Hewitt, "Scribbler's Letter to Gustavus," *LHJ*, No. 2, September 1885, p. 6.

25. Editorial Notes, "Why They Do Not Marry" *LHJ*, July 1985, p. 4.

26. Anonymous "Married and Settled," *LHJ*, March 1885, p. 4.

27. Fannie L. Fancher, "Aunt Melissa's Mission," *LHJ*, July 1885, p. 2.

28. Ibid.

29. Patricia Searles and Janet Mickish, "A Thoroughbred Girl: Images of Female Gender Roles in Turn-of-the-Century Mass Media," *Women's Studies* 3 (1984), p. 262.

30. "Editorial Notes" *LHJ*, March 1885, p. 4. These incomes were quite enormous for the day. According to Claudia Goldin, most male professionals of the day earned far less. *Understanding the Gender Gap*, pp. 64–65.

31. "Editorial Notes" *LHJ*, April 1885, p. 4.

32. "A Day with Ida Lewis," by Ellen Le Garde, *LHJ*, July 1890, pp. 1–2.

33. Felicia Holt "A Woman's Plea for Woman," Editorial, *LHJ*, October 1889, p. 10.

34. Lee Virginia Chambers-Schiller, *Liberty a Better Husband: Single Women in America: The Generations of 1780–1840* (New Haven: Yale University Press, 1984).

35. Edward Bok, "Women Who Are Uncrowned Heroines," *LHJ*, July 1890, p. 10.

36. "A Girl's Life at Vassar" by a Vassar Girl, July 1890, p. 7.

37. The *Journal* did not serve up any regular material on collegiate women in its first years. I found few pieces, fictional or otherwise, with a focus on college-educated woman, although the first editor, Louisa Knapp, clearly supported education for women. She advocated that parents "educate . . . girls as well as . . . boys to be self-supporting" and urged "young ladies" to become "proficient in some one thing, so that you can earn your own living, should it be necessary or should you wish to do so," *LHJ*, February 1984, p. 2.

Moreover, while laudatory characterizations of real, unmarried working women did appear between 1883 and 1890, most of the fictional spinsters who appeared in the magazine's first decade were relatively uneducated. These maiden aunts and timid celibates, as befitted their often retiring if sometimes self-involved dispositions, generally appeared in auxiliary roles in other people's stories.

38. Bok edited the *Journal* from October 1889 through October 1916.

39. According to Mabel Newcomer, 1.9 percent of women aged 18 to 21 attended college in 1880 and that proportion increased only to 2.2 percent in 1890. The proportions of 18 to 21-year-old women attending college almost doubled between 1890 and 1910 and then doubled in the ensuing decade to 7.6 percent in 1920. *A Century of Higher Education for American Women* (New York: Harper, 1959), p. 46.

40. Ruth Freeman and Patricia Klaus, "Blessed or Not? The New Spinster in England and the United States in the Late Nineteenth and Early Twentieth Centuries," *Journal of Family History* (Winter 1984), pp. 394–414. Freeman and Klaus cite articles published in both the United States and Britain. In the United States, they found such articles in *Good Housekeeping* (1911), *Harper's Bazaar* (1907), *Scribner's* (1915, 1917, and 1922), and *American Magazine* (1919). Freeman and Klaus use these pieces to describe the actual lives of "bachelor women" and to argue that "the new spinsters . . . helped to reverse traditional scorn for old maids and to pave the way for those who would later demand, like men, to combine work and marriage." In contrast, I see them less as reflections of reality than as claims-making documents.

41. This was a common feature of such pieces; Klaus and Freeman's (1984) bibliography lists a number of autobiographical articles that appeared in these years in Britain and the United States with authors who titled themselves similarly (e.g., "A Bachelor Maid," "One of the Sisterhood," "An Old Maid That Needs No Apology").

42. Francesca Polletta, " 'It Was Like a Fever . . .' Narrative and Identity in Social Protest," *Social Problems* (1998), 45:(2), p. 142.

43. An Old Maid, "Why I Never Married," *LHJ*, November 1890, p. 4.

44. Ibid.

45. "The Story of Five Proposals," signed "Phyllis Perchance," *LHJ*, July 1893, pp. 1–2. In the October 1893 issue, Edward Bok identified the author as Lilian Bell,

one of "Four Clever Young Literary Women," author of "The Love Affairs of an Old Maid," and of "the 'Story of Five Proposals,' one of the most successful ever published in this magazine, signed by the clever nom de plume of Phyllis Perchance (p. 5).

46. A Spinster Who Has Learned to Say No, "The Three Men Who Asked Me to Marry Them," *LHJ*, October 1913, p. 70.

47. Ibid.

48. An Old Maid, "Why I Never Married."

49. Anonymous "Why They Do Not Marry," *LHJ*, July 1885, p. 4.

50. Margaret Harvey, "Advice to Young Women Who Are Alone in the World," *LHJ*, October 1885, p. 2.

51. A Spinster Who Has Learned to Say No, "The Three Men Who Asked Me to Marry Them," *LHJ*.

CHAPTER FOUR

1. *Ladies' Home Journal*, December 1913, pp. 7, 8, 50.

2. See entry in *Who's Who in America* (Chicago: Marquis Publishing, 1914).

CHAPTER FIVE

1. Jessie Bernard, *Academic Women* (University Park, PA: State University Press, 1964); Mary Walsh, *Doctors Wanted, No Women Need Apply: Barriers in the Medical Profession, 1835–1975* (New Haven: Yale University Press, 1977); Regina Morantz-Sanchez, *Sympathy and Science: Women Physicians in American Medicine* (Oxford: Oxford University Press, 1985).

2. Proportions rose from 1 percent in 1890 to 6 percent in 1900, to 11 percent in 1910, to 15 percent in 1920, and finally to a high of 18 percent in 1930. In 1940, only 13 percent of doctorates were granted to women and by 1950 the proportion was down to 10 percent. Patricia Albjerg Graham, "Expansion and Exclusion: A History of Women in American Higher Education," *Signs: Journal of Women in Culture and Society* (3:4, 1978), p. 766.

3. Barbara Solomon, *In the Company of Educated Women* (New Haven: Yale University Press, 1985), chapter 5. In *Killing the Spirit: Higher Education in America* (New York: Penguin Books, 1990), p. 67, Page Smith notes that, as late as 1900, only 2.3 percent of youth of college age were enrolled as candidates for the bachelor's degree in institutions of higher education. Solomon describes female collegians as coming from the most socially mobile families within the expanding middle classes.

4. In the period between 1890 and 1920, women constituted 20 percent of college faculties and close to 30 percent in the decade before 1940. After that, numbers of female faculty declined precipitously. Graham, "Expansion and Exclusion: A History of Women in American Higher Education"; Jessie Bernard, *Academic Women* (University Park, PA: State University Press, 1964), p 138, says that most women on college faculties were spinsters. Solomon (*In the Company of Educated Women*) cites an AAUW study that found 75 percent of the women who had earned Ph.D. before 1924 were unmarried.

Even in the mid-1920s, only half of the women Ph.Ds surveyed combined marriage and career.

5. Barbara Solomon, *In the Company of Educated Women,* p. 118.

6. Carl Degler, *At Odds: American from the Revolution to the Present* (New York: Oxford University Press, 1980), p. 164.

7. Carl N. Degler, *At Odds,* p. 385.

8. Barbara Sicherman, "College and Careers: Historical Perspectives on the Life and Work Patterns of Women College Graduates," in *Women and Higher Education in American,* ed. by John Faragher and Florence Howe (New York: W.W. Norton, 1990), pp. 130–164; Mary E. Cookingham, "Combining Marriage, Motherhood and Jobs Before World War II: Women College Graduates, Classes of 1909–1934." *Journal of Family History* (9:2, 1984).

9. Morantz-Sanchez, *Sympathy and Science,* 1985.

10. Claudia Goldin, *Understanding the Gender Gap: An Economic History of American Women* (New York: Oxford University Press, 1990).

11. Sheila M. Rothman, *Woman's Proper Place: A History of Changing Ideals and Practices, 1870 to the Present* (New York: Basic Books, 1978).

12. *Inarticulate Longings* (New York: Routledge, 1995), p. 82.

13. Patricia Searles and Janet Mickish, "A Thoroughbred Girl: Images of Female Gender Roles in Turn-of-the-Century Mass Media," *Women's Studies* 10, 1984, pp. 261–281.

14. Carroll Smith-Rosenberg, "The New Woman as Androgyne: Social Disorder and Gender Crisis, 1870–1936," in *Disorderly Conduct: Visions of Gender in Victorian America* (New York: Oxford University Press, 1985), pp. 245–296.

15. "Somebody's Spinster" by Emily Meigs Ripley, *LHJ,* March 1993, p. 8.

16. William Leach, *True Love and Perfect Union: The Feminist Reform of Sex and Society* (Middletown: Weslyan University Press, 1989), chapter 8.

17. Bok was not alone in these concerns. His effusions were contributions to the larger debate about the "new woman" described by Caroll Smith-Rosenberg in "The New Woman as Androgyne: Social Disorder and Gender Crisis, 1870–1936."

18. April, 1893, "Home with the Editor."

19. The speech "Woman's Part in the Future" was delivered at the anniversary of the founding of Mount Holyoke College.

20. Glenna Matthews, *The Rise of Public Woman: Woman's Power and Woman's Place in the United States, 1630–1970* (New York: Oxford University Press, 1992). Introduction. According to Amanda Frisken, Victoria Woodhull, the quintessential female rebel of the "gilded age," did try to take on the label. Her resulting notoriety substantiates Matthews's claim. See "Sexual Politics in Reconstruction: The Woodhull Years, 1970–1876," unpublished dissertation, Department of History, State University of New York/ Stony Brook, 1999.

21. See Degler, *At Odds,* pp. 150–160 and Sicherman, "College and Careers."

22. Theodore Roosevelt, quoted in Linda Gordon, *Woman's Body, Woman's Right: Birth Control in America* (New York: Penguin Books, 1977), chapter 7.

23. Based on census data for numbers of single women aged 45–54 in each decennial census year, rates of spinsterhood were highest for the cohort of women born between 1866 and 1875. This cohort of women would have reached marriageable age somewhere between 1884 and 1905. The figures, as estimated from census data, follow.

Census Year	Birth Dates of Women Aged 45–54 during the Year	Percent Never Married
1890	1836–45	7.1
1900	1846–65	7.8
1910	1856–75	8.5
1920	1866–85	9.5
1930	1876–85	9.1
1940	1886–95	8.7
1950	1896–05	7.8
1960	1906–15	7.0
1970	1916–25	5.5
1980	1926–35	4.7
1990	1936–45	5.0

Derived from *Historical Statistics of the United States, Colonial Times to 1970* (Washington: U.S. Department of Commerce, Bureau of the Census, 1976), Series A 160–171, pp. 20–21, and *Statistical Abstract of the United States* (Washington: U.S. Department of Commerce, Bureau of the Census), 1992, Table 51, p 45. Moreover, as demographer Mary Jo Bane demonstrates, the average age at marriage for American women was 22 in 1890. The average age then dropped steadily thereafter to a low of 20 in the mid-1950s. *Here to Stay* (New York: Basic Books, 1976), p. 23.

24. Frank Dikotter, "Race Culture: Recent Perspectives on the History of Eugenics," *American Historical Review*, (10:2, 1998), p. 468.

25. *Horrible Prettiness: Burlesque and American Culture* (Chapel Hill: University of North Carolina Press, 1991), pp. 26–27.

26. Robert C. Allen, *Horrible Prettiness*, p. 30.

27. As Judith Butler noted in her seminal work, *Gender Trouble: Feminism and the Subversion of Identity* (New York: Routledge, 1990), chapter 3, a "dissonant juxtaposition" of what is defined as masculine and feminine may ultimately function to destabilize "both as they come into erotic interplay." In burlesque, through the mechanism of drag performance, "the original" as Butler argues, could be "revealed to be a copy, and an inevitably failed one." Such attacks were thus not merely misogynist, they attacked dominant definitions of the elements of respectability; through parody of some of the most vulnerable of their "betters," women who, by virtue of their vaunted independence, lacked secure male protection.

28. Sharon R. Ullman, *Sex Seen: The Emergence of Modern Sexuality in America* (Berkeley: University of California Press, 1997), pp. 20–23. In *Screening Out the Past: The Birth of Mass Culture and the Motion Picture Industry* (Chicago: University of Chicago Press, 1983), Lary May describes movies in this period as a working-class entertainment.

29. Amelia E. Barr, "Why Do Not Literary Women Marry?" *LHJ*, November 1893, p. 10.

30. Ibid.

31. Ella Wheeler Wilcox, "The Happy Woman," *LHJ*, March 1889, p. 24.

32. "Accommodating Protest: Working Women, the New Veiling, and Change in Cairo," *Signs: Journal of Women in Culture and Society*, (20:1, 1994).

33. "Comment on Fraser and Gordon's 'A Genealogy of Dependency': Tracing a Keyword of the U.S. Welfare State," *Signs: Journal of Women in Culture and Society* (21:2, 1996), pp. 515–530.

CHAPTER SIX

1. On the importance of this audience, see Jennifer Scanlon's book *Inarticulate Longings: The Ladies' Home Journal, Gender, and the Promises of Consumer Cultures*, p. 41. For a discussion of the changing situation of college girls, see Patricia Albjerg Graham, "Expansion and Exclusion: A History of Women in American Higher Education." *Signs: Journal of Women in Culture and Society* (3:4, 1978), pp. 759–773.

2. *Ladies' Home Journal*, March 1933, pp. 5–7, 100, 103.

CHAPTER SEVEN

1. She might well have been enjoying her summer vacation when General Douglas MacArthur ignored President Hoover's orders, sent his troops into the Anacostia Flats shantytown built by the Bonus Marchers, and ordered the soldiers to use tear gas bombs to prevent what he viewed as the start of a revolution.

2. According to her obituary, Montross did not give up on either career or marriage. She married again and continued to produce short stories and novels for commercial gain. "Lois Montross Is Dead at 64; Novelist and Magazine Writer," *New York Times*, September 18, 1961, p. 29.

3. Jennifer Scanlon, *Inarticulate Longings: The Ladies' Home Journal, Gender, and the Promises of Consumer Culture* (New York: Routledge, 1995), p. 93.

4. See Mary Cookingham, "Combining Marriage, Motherhood and Jobs Before World War II: Women College Graduates, Classes of 1909–1934." *Journal of Family History* (9:2, 1984), pp. 178–195, and Claudia Goldin, *Understanding the Gender Gap: An Economic History of American Women* (New York: Oxford University Press, 1990), chapter 5.

5. Frank Stricker, "Cookbooks and Law Books: The Hidden History of Career Women in Twentieth Century America," *Journal of Social History* (10:1, 1976), pp. 1–19.

6. Claudia Goldin, *Understanding the Gender Gap*, p. 16.

7. Jointly conducted by the *Journal* and the National Council of Women for presentation at the Century of Progress Exposition at Chicago, the "poll" was accomplished through voluntary submission. In its writeup of the results, the magazine proudly announced that over 128,000 "ballots" had been cast in the poll. The top twelve names were: Mary Baker Eddy, Jane Addams, Clara Barton, Frances E. Willard, Susan B. Anthony, Hellen Keller, Harriet Beecher Stowe, Julia Ward Howe, Carrie Chapman Catt, Amelia Earhart Putnam, Mary Lyon, and Mary E. Woolley. "Twelve and a Thirteenth," *LHJ*, March 1933, p. 24.

8. This piece is, for example, close to a complete reprise of one published by the magazine in January 1923. A similar effort, to determine the twelve greatest living women, had provided at least one earlier edition of the magazine with the opportunity to draw a parallel between the "The Unknown Soldier" of the (then) recent world war and what was construed as the exemplar of excellence in womanhood. That piece, "The

Unknown Great American Woman: Not a Singer, Nor a Writer, Nor a Musician, But a Simple Back-Country Mother," written by Corra Harris, called for the recognition of America's "greatest woman," the mother who "never had anything, and . . . has given everything," who "made a home," and "produced brave men for its defense."

9. April 1933, p. 16.

10. "Has Her Cake and Eats it Too, *LHJ*, August 1933, p. 8.

11. "Business Women in Love," *LHJ*, June 1933, p. 5.

12. "Business Women in Love," p. 80.

13. "The Case of Dr. Crawford," *LHJ*, November 1933, p. 5.

14. Barbara Levy Simon, *Never Married Women* (Philadelphia: Temple University Press, 1987), p. 13. In *The Spinster and Her Enemies: Feminism and Sexuality, 1880–1930* (London: Pandora, 1985), Sheila Jeffreys discusses the consequences of transformation in ideas about sexuality for unmarried women in Britain.

15. For Mason's revisionist view, see his book, *The Making of Victorian Sexuality* (Oxford: Oxford University Press), 1995.

16. Carolyn J. Dean, *Sexuality and Modern Western Culture* (New York: Twayne, 1996), pp. 2–5, 33.

17. See especially Steven Seidman, *Romantic Longings: Love in America, 1830–1980* (New York: Routledge, 1991), chapter 3, and John D'Emilio and Estelle B. Freedman, *Intimate Matters: A History of Sexuality in America* (New York: Harper & Row, 1988), chapter 10.

18. For more detailed discussions of this process, see *Inventing the Psychological: Toward a Cultural History of Emotional Life in American*, edited by Joel Pfister and Nancy Schnog (New Haven: Yale University Press), 1997.

19. Seidman, *Romantic Longings.*

20. Lillian Faderman, *Surpassing the Love of Men* (New York: Morrow, 1981).

21. M. Esther Harding, *The Way of All Women: A Psychological Interpretation* (New York: Longmans, 1934), p. 224.

22. Sheila Jeffreys, author of *The Spinster and Her Enemies,* is one of the most notable exponents of this point of view, but her work focuses exclusively on the British context. However, Lillian Faderman's discussion of sexology in *Surpassing the Love of Men* and Carrol Smith-Rosenberg's depiction of attacks on the "new woman" in *Disorderly Conduct: Visions of Gender in Victorian America: Visions of Gender in Victorian America* (Oxford: Oxford University Press, 1985) describe a similar set of processes in the United States. For a more developed discussion of this perspective see Alison Oram's article, "Repressed and Thwarted, or Bearer of the New World? The Spinster in Inter-war Feminist Discourses," *Women's History Review* (1:3, 1992), pp. 413–434.

23. Leila J. Rupp, "Sexuality and Politics in the Early Twentieth Century: The Case of the International Women's Movement," *Feminist Studies* (23:3, 1997), p. 578.

24. Jeffreys, *The Spinster and Her Enemies,* p. 175.

25. Laura Doan, *Old Maids to Radical Spinsters: Unmarried Women in the Twentieth-Century Novel* (Urbana: University of Illinois Press, 1991), p. 4.

26. Katharine Bement Davis, *Factors in the Sex life of Twenty-two Hundred Women* (New York: Harper and Brothers, 1929), p. xx. The second wave of a larger study, this nonrandom study of single women conducted in the early 1920s is one of the few numerative sources on the sex lives of unmarried women before the Kinsey studies. The 1,200 unmarried respondents surveyed were all college graduates who had been out of college at least five years. Their average age was 37, with a range of 22–68.

27. Robert Latou Dickinson and Lura Beam, *The Single Woman: A Medical Study in Sex Education* (New York: Reynal & Hitchcock, 1934), p. xiii. This data, derived from physicians' records, focused on women who had been seen for treatment. The records included women from a wider range of socioeconomic groupings than the Davis study, but it also contained some significant numbers of women still in their teens. Because it was drawn from medical records that had been collected (largely by Dr. Dickinson), the study provides far less systematic information than did Davis's. However, this study found that one out of seven of the 650 single women in the records was not a "virgin."

28. Dickinson and Beam, *The Single Woman*, p. 108.

29. Ibid.

30. Dickinson and Beam, *The Single Woman*, p. 282. The researchers also included two women who were "mental defectives" in the chapter, but unlike the other women who were described here, they were "not-virgin."

31. Ibid.

32. Margaret Adams, *Single Blessedness: Observations on the Single Status in Married Society* (New York: Basic Books, 1976). Adams grew up in England but her book was about singles in the United States. Contrasting her own (English) past and the American present she says:

> rapid changes in sexual mores and a greater flexibility and variety in personal relationships are relentlessly rubbing out (or at least blurring) the sharply drawn lines that formerly separated the social status and behavior of those who were married from those who had not embraced this state; these changes have created all sorts of marital and sexual configurations that defy neat categorization.

Adams' respondents were rather more diverse than the unmarried career women of her youth. She interviewed several young feminists who had decided to embrace celibacy as a way of avoiding male dominance. She also decided to include women who had once been married but were presently living as singles. In the end, childlessness rather than marital status, age, *or* sexual abstinence became her criterion for inclusion.

33. Harding, *The Way of All Women*, p. 253–234.

34. Harding, *The Way of All Women*, pp. 231 and 253.

35. Laura Hutton's book, *The Single Woman and her Emotional Problems*, was first published in London by Bailliere, Tindall and Cox in 1935. Having sold well, it was reissued by the same firm in an expanded and revised edition in 1937. Although the references in Hutton's book were primarily British, the book found a wide audience both in Europe and the United States; an updated and revised edition was printed in New York by Roy Publishers in 1960.

36. Hutton, *The Single Woman and Her Emotional Problems*, chapter 4.

37. Ibid., chapter 1.

38. Ibid., p. 10.

39. Benjamin B. Wolman, editor (New York: Holt, 1996).

40. See especially Thomas Laqueur, *Making Sex: Body and Gender from the Greeks to Freud* (Cambridge: Harvard University Press, 1990) and the collection edited by Roger N. Lancaster and Micaela di Leonardo, *The Gender Sexuality Reader* (New York: Routledge, 1997).

41. Judith Butler, *Gender Trouble: Feminism and the Subversion of Identity* (New York: Routledge, 1990), p. 112.

42. See Seidman, *Romantic Longings,* D'Emilio and Freedman, *Intimate Matters,* and Faderman, *Surpassing the Love of Women.*

43. Mary Jo Deegan, " 'DEAR LOVE, DEAR LOVE,' Feminist Pragmatism and the Chicago Female World of Love and Ritual," in *Gender and Society* (10:5, 1996), p. 593.

44. "Skis and Doughnuts" by Stephen W. Meader, *LHJ,* January 1933, pp. 10 and 44.

45. "The Flaming Gahagans" a serialized story by Helen Topping Miller, *LHJ,* March (p. 3)–July 1933.

CHAPTER EIGHT

1. Directed by Frank Capra and released just after the end of the war in 1946, the film celebrated the nation's victory by creating a dystopic vision of the world without the everyday virtues of its citizenry. Bailey, as played by Jimmy Stewart, is the kind of independent and morally courageous everyman who sacrifices himself and his ambitions to protect family and community against the forces of avarice and despotism. Like his country, he is threatened, but ultimately vindicated.

2. Marjorie Rosen, *Popcorn Venus: Women, Movies and the American Dream* (New York: Coward, McCann and Geoghegan, 1973).

3. Jackie Byars, *All That Hollywood Allows: Re-Reading Gender in 1950s Melodrama* (Chapel Hill: University of North Carolina Press, 1991), pp. 91–92. Byars may be right about the effect of such portrayals, but the evidence described in this chapter suggests that she was incorrect about their timing.

4. Alice Kessler-Harris, *Out to Work: A History of Wage Earning Women in the United States* (New York: Oxford University Press, 1982), chapter 10.

5. Gertrude Schweitzer, "The Doctor Is a Woman," *LHJ,* April 1943.

6. William H. Chafe, *The American Woman: Her Changing Social, Economic, and Political Roles, 1920–1970* (New York: Oxford University Press, 1972), p. 218. For specification of some of the particularities of women's expanding labor force participation in the postwar epoch, see also *Understanding the Gender Gap: An Economic History of American Women* (New York: Oxford University Press, 1990), by Claudia Goldin; *Not June Cleaver: Women and Gender in Postwar American, 1945–1960,* edited by Joanne Meyerowitz (Philadelphia: Temple University Press, 1994) and Valerie K. Oppenheimer's book, *The Female Labor Force in the United States,* Population Monograph Series, no. 5 (Berkeley: University of California Press, 1970).

7. See especially Andrew Cherlin, *Marriage, Divorce, Remarriage* (Cambridge: Harvard University Press, 1981); D. A. Ahlburg and C. J. De Vita, "New Realities of the American Family," *Population Bulletin,* 47 (2) (Washington, D.C.: Population Reference Bureau, 1992); and Mary Jo Bane, *Here to Stay: American Families in the Twentieth Century* (New York: Basic Books, 1976).

8. William Chafe, *The Unfinished Journey: America Since World War II,* 4th ed. (New York: Oxford University Press, 1998), p. 123.

9. *LHJ,* April 1953, p. 28.

10. About half of the female respondents in Alfred Kinsey's landmark 1953 study, *Sexual Behavior in the Human Female,* had engaged in premarital sexual activity.

11. Steven Seidman, *Romantic Longings: Love in America, 1830–1980* (New York: Routledge, 1991), p. 125.

12. William B. Faherty, S.J., *Living Alone: A Guide for the Single Woman* (New York: Sheed and Ward, 1964), p. 42. See also McCauley, Laurence James, *The Single Woman* (New York: Duell, Sloan and Pearce, 1952).

13. Apparently, the cultural environment was such that spinsters appeared to be at least as numerous to one academic as they had been in any previous period. In 1951, Dorothy Deegan, a sociologist writing about the representation of spinsters in American novels, described it as a rampant condition, beginning her book (*The Stereotype of the Single Woman in American Novels: A Social Study with Implications for the Education of Women*) depicting spinsterhood as an ongoing social problem. She said:

> Since early colonial days in American, single women have gradually become a perceptible group in the population, until today they are numbered in millions and comprise a significant minority. The fact that so many women—strong, healthy, attractive, and superior women—do not or cannot marry creates a problem which is both sociological and psychological. . . . Their place in a society founded upon monogamous marriage is one of far-reaching importance, and their problem of personal adjustment, by reason of deviating from that pattern, is beginning to be recognized as sharing unique components.

14. The employed spinsters were: the perennially harassed secretary of a wealthy woman, a motherly clerk who functioned as the personnel officer in a government office, a "starchy" chief nurse, a dressmaker who fostered her young neighbor and helped her to find a marriage partner, and a "straight and strong" countrywoman "with big, bony hands" and piercing vision who helped her socialite neighbor adjust to married life. These characters appeared in the following stories: Phillis Bottome, "Survival" (serialized in several issues); Adela Rogers St. Johns, "Government Girl," January 1943 (serialized); "Navy Nurse," 1943 (serialized); Mildred Cain, "Intimate Strangers," May 1943; Charlotte Edwards, "Beauty's Right," June 1943.

15. Margaret Carpenter, "Experiment Perilous," *LHJ*, July 1943, "The Doctor Is a Woman," and Anya Seton's serialized story "Dragonwyck."

16. Ferdinand Lundberg and Marynia F. Farnham, *Modern Woman: The Lost Sex* (New York: Harper & Bros, 1947); see especially pp. 19 and 381.

17. Lundberg and Farnham, *Modern Woman*, p. 120.

18. Lundberg and Farnham, *Modern Woman*, pp. 364–365.

19. See Tania Modleski's discussion of the "woman's genre" in "A Woman's Gotta Do . . . What a Man's Gotta Do? Cross-Dressing in the Western," *Signs* (22:3, 1997), pp. 519–544, and Stanley Cavell, *Contesting Tears: The Hollywood Melodrama of the Unknown Woman* (Chicago: University of Chicago Press, 1992).

20. Her vocational choice is especially telling, given the context—she embarks on the construction of lurid romances for the genre of "true confessions" magazines.

21. *Dramas, Fields, Metaphors: Symbolic Action in Human Society* (Ithaca: Cornell University Press, 1974).

22. *Now, Voyager,* was based on a 1941 novel of the same title written by Olive Prouty (New York: Random House). *Summertime* was based on a 1951 play by Arthur Laurents called *Time of the Cuckoo.*

23. Graeme Turner, *Film as Social Practice* (London: Routledge, 1993), p. 78.

24. Under the studio system, films became "layered collective enterprises"— they were developed, produced, and distributed by a host of participants. Made to make money, they were designed, cast, and marketed to appeal to as wide a swath of viewers

as possible. Yet few cinematic productions actually achieved the popularity that their makers hoped for; filmmakers and their backers frequently misestimated what the public will appreciate. Indeed, a film's success seems to have depended less on the conscious ploys of its makers than on happenstance.

For every high-grossing success, a substantial number of bombs were issued. Although the allure of making a movie that would engage a far-flung audience and gross a fortune has long lured aspiring filmmakers and financiers into the industry, the ability to accurately gauge those themes, personae, and devices that will attract prospective viewers has remained elusive. Charismatic actors, canny producers, directors with long track records, brilliant scriptwriters, and sophisticated surveys failed as often as they succeeded in predicting what would sell and what wouldn't.

25. Although Charlotte Vale's age is not specified in either book or movie, she is presented as young enough to have children and yet old enough to look dumpy, fat, and middle-aged.

26. *Contesting Tears: The Hollywood Melodrama of the Unknown Woman* (Chicago: University of Chicago Press, 1996), p. 117.

27. *A Fine Romance: Five Ages of Film Feminism* (Philadelphia: Temple University Press, 1995). Thus, Mellencamp argues, Hitchcock indicates a female character's narrative enigma by hiding her in glasses.

28. Originally written for the *New York Journal,* the piece was reprinted in the *Ladies Home Journal* in February 1897. A portion has been reprinted in *Magazines for the Millions: Gender and Commerce in the Ladies' Home Journal and the Saturday Evening Post 1880–1910* by Helen Damon-Moore (New York: State University of New York Press, 1994), pp. 32–33.

29. E. Ann Kaplan, "The Case of the Missing Mother" in *Issues in Feminist Film Criticism,* ed. by Patricia Ehrens (Bloomington: Indiana University Press, 1990), p. 128.

30. Nina Farrell, *Every Girl Is Entitled to a Husband* (New York: McGraw-Hill), pp. 2, 6, 196.

31. In her analysis, Kozol cites, as do others, the chilling depictions of destructive motherhood in Phillip Wylie's 1942 best seller, *Generation of Vipers* and the 1955 movie classic, *Rebel Without a Cause.*

32. Betty Friedan, *The Feminine Mystique* (New York: Norton, 1963) and William McNeil, *Everyone Was Brave: A History of Feminism in America,* (Chicago: Quadrangle Books, 1969).

33. The first chapter of Jackie Byars' book, *All That Hollywood Allows: Re-reading Gender in 1950s Melodrama* (Chapel Hill: University of North Carolina Press, 1991), contains an excellent discussion of the history of feminist film criticism.

34. May, *Homeward Bound,* pp. 53–54.

35. *Young White and Miserable: Growing Up Female in the Fifties* (Boston: Beacon Press, 1992), p. 11. See also Elaine Tyler May, "Explosive Issues," in *Recasting America: Culture and Politics in the Age of the Cold War,* ed. by Lary May (Chicago: University of Chicago Press, 1989) and *Homeward Bound: American Families in the Cold War Era* (New York: Basic Books, 1987).

CHAPTER NINE

1. Hazel Markus and Paula Nurius, "Possible Selves," in *American Psychologist* (41:9, 1986), pp. 954–969.

2. Janet Todd, *Women and Film* (New York: Holmes and Meier, 1988).

3. Barbara M. Solomon, *In the Company of Educated Women: A History of Women and Higher Education in America* (New Haven: Yale University Press, 1985), chapter 12.

4. Claudia Goldin, *Understanding the Gender Gap: An Economic History of American Women* (New York: Oxford University Press, 1990), p. 203.

5. See Adrienne Rich, "Compulsory Heterosexuality and Lesbian Existence," *Signs* (5:4, 1981), pp. 713–736.

6. "Beyond the Feminine Mystique," in *Not June Cleaver: Women and Gender in Postwar America, 1945–1960,* ed. by Joanne Meyerowitz (Philadelphia: Temple University Press, 1994), p. 231

7. According to the Women's Research and Education Institute, by 1994 one-quarter of all families with children under eighteen years of age in the United States were maintained by women (up from 15 percent in 1975). Moreover, by the mid-1990s, most mothers were in the labor force. Seventy-six percent of women with children age six to seventeen, 60 percent of women with children under six, and over half of women with children under age one were "active in the labor market" in 1994. *The American Woman 1996–97: Women and Work,* ed. by Cynthia Costello and Barbara Kivimae Krimgold (New York: W.W. Norton, 1996), p. 55.

8. Wini Breines, *Young, White and Miserable: Growing up Female in the Fifties* (Boston: Beacon Press, 1992), chapter 1.

9. Barbara Ehrenreich, *The Hearts of Men* (Garden City, New York: Doubleday, 1983).

10. "Virtual Truth with a Vengeance," in *Contemporary Sociology* Symposium, "Half-Truths with Real Consequences: Journalism, Research and Public Policy" (28:2, 1999), p. 19.

11. "Femininity as Discourse," in *Becoming Feminine: The Politics of Popular Culture*" ed. by Leslie G. Roman and Linda K. Christian-Smith (Philadelphia: Falmer Press, 1988), pp. 37–59.

BIBLIOGRAPHY

Adams, Margaret. *Single Blessedness: Observations on the Single Status in Married Society.* New York: Basic Books, 1976.

Ahlburg, D. A., and C. J. De Vita. "New Realities of the American Family." *Population Bulletin*, 47 (2). Washington, DC: Population Reference Bureau, 1992.

Allen, Robert C. *Horrible Prettiness: Burlesque and American Culture.* Chapel Hill: University of North Carolina Press, 1991.

Ang, Jen. "Feminist Desire and Feminist Pleasure: On Janice Radway's *Reading the Romance: Women, Patriarchy and Popular Literature.*" *Camera Obscura* 16 (1988), pp. 134–176.

Auerbach, Nina. *Our Vampires Ourselves.* Chicago: University of Chicago Press, 1995.

Bane, Mary Jo. *Here to Stay.* New York: Basic Books, 1976.

Bernard, Jessie. *Academic Women.* University Park, PA: State University Press, 1964.

Bohannon, Laura. "Shakespeare in the Bush." In Johnetta B. Cole, ed., *Anthropology for the Eighties.* New York: Free Press, 1982.

Breines, Wini. *Young, White annd Miserable: Growing Up Female in the Fifties.* Boston: Beacon Press, 1992.

Butler, Judith. *Gender Trouble: Feminism and the Subversion of Identity.* New York: Routledge, 1990.

Byars, Jackie. *All That Hollywood Allows: Re-reading Gender in 1950s Melodrama.* Chapel Hill: University of North Carolina Press, 1991.

Cavell, Stanley. *Contesting Tears: The Hollywood Melodrama of the Unknown Woman.* Chicago: University of Chicago Press, 1996.

Chafe, William. *The Unfinished Journey: America Since World War II*, 4th ed. New York: Oxford University Press, 1998.

Chambers-Schiller, Lee Virginia. " 'Woman is Born to Love': The Maiden Aunt as Maternal Figure in Ante-bellum Literature." *Frontiers* 10:1 (1988), pp. 34–43.

———. *Liberty a Better Husband: Single Women in America: The Generations of 1780–1840.* New Haven: Yale University Press, 1984.

Cherlin, Andrew. *Marriage, Divorce, Remarriage.* Cambridge: Harvard University Press, 1981.

Christie, Agatha. *Murder on the Orient Express.* New York: Dodd Mead, 1968 [1934].

Clinton, Catherine. *The Other Civil War: American Women in the Nineteenth Century.* New York: Hill and Wang, 1984.

Cookingham, Mary E. "Combining Marriage, Motherhood and Jobs Before World War II: Women College Graduates, Classes of 1909–1934." *Journal of Family History* 9:2 (1984), pp. 178–195.

Costello, Cynthia, and Barbara Kivimae Krimgold, eds., *The American Woman 1996–97: Women and Work*, Women's Research and Education Institute. New York: W.W. Norton, 1996.

Cott, Nancy. "Passionlessness: An Interpretation of Victorian Sexual Ideology, 1790–1850," in *Signs: Journal of Women in Culture and Society,* 4:2 (1978), pp. 219–236.

———. *The Bonds of Womanhood: Woman's "Sphere" in New England, 1780–1835.* New Haven: Yale University Press, 1977.

Cowie, Elizabeth. *Representing the Woman: Cinema and Psychoanalysis.* Minneapolis: University of Minnesota Press, 1997.

Curle, Richard. *Women: An Analytic Study.* London: Watts & Co.

Currie, Dawn H. "Decoding Femininity: Advertisements and Their Teenage Readers." *Gender and Society* 11:4 (1997), pp. 453–477.

Damon-Moore, Helen. *Magazines for the Millions: Gender and Commerce in the Ladies' Home Journal and the Saturday Evening Post 1880–1910.* Albany: State University of New York Press, 1994.

Davies, Marjorie. *Woman's Place is at the Typewriter: Office Work and Office Workers 1870–1930.* Philadelphia: Temple University Press, 1982.

D'Emilio, John, and Estelle B. Freedman. *Intimate Matters: A History of Sexuality in America.* New York: Harper & Row, 1988.

Dean, Carolyn J. *Sexuality and Modern Western Culture.* New York: Twayne, 1996.

Deegan, Dorthy Yost. *The Stereotype of the Single Woman in American Novels: A Social Study with Implications for the Education of Women.* New York: Kings Crown Press, 1951.

Deegan, Mary Jo. "DEAR LOVE, DEAR LOVE" Feminist Pragmatism and the Chicago Female World of Love and Ritual. *Gender and Society* 10:5 (1996), pp. 590–607.

Degler, Carl N. *At Odds: Women and the Family in American from the Revolution to the Present.* Oxford: Oxford University Press, 1980.

Delaney, Sarah, and A. Elizabeth, with Amy Hill. *Having Our Say: The Delaney Sisters' First One Hundred Years.* Heath, New York: Kodansha International, 1993.

Deutsch, Helene. *The Psychology of Women: A Psychoanalytic Interpretation*, vol. 1. New York: Grune & Stratton, 1944.

Dikotter, Frank. "Race Culture: Recent Perspectives on the History of Eugenics." *American Historical Review* 10: 2 (1998), pp. 467–478.

Doan, Laura L., ed. *Old Maids to Radical Spinsters: Unmarried Women in the Twentieth-Century Novel.* Urbana: University of Illinois Press, 1991.

Doyle, Arthur Conan. "The Silver Blaze" [originally published in *Strand Magazine*, 1892] in *The Adventures of Sherlock Holmes*, ed. by Edgar W. Smith. New York: The Heritage Press, 1950, pp. 515–539.

DuBois, Ellen ed. *Elizabeth Cady Stanton, Susan B. Anthony: Correspondence, Writings, Speeches.* New York: Schocken Books, 1981.

Ehrenreich, Barbara. *The Hearts of Men.* Garden City, New York: Doubleday, 1983.

Faderman, Lillian. *Surpassing the Love of Men.* New York: Morrow, 1981.

Faherty, S.J., William B. *Living Alone: A Guide for the Single Woman.* New York: Sheed and Ward, 1964.

Farrell, Nina. *Every Girl Is Entitled to a Husband.* New York: McGraw-Hill, 1963.

Forester, C. S. *The African Queen.* London: Penguin, 1935.

Foucault, Michel. *The History of Sexuality, Volume 1: An Introduction.* Robert Hurley, translator. New York: Pantheon, 1978.

Freed, Richard M. *Nightmare in Red: Disloyalty in American Politics.* New York: Oxford University Press, 1990.

Freeman, Ruth, and Patricia Klaus. "Blessed or Not? The New Spinster in England and the United States in the Late Nineteenth and Early Twentieth Centuries." *Journal of Family History 9:2* (1984), pp. 394–415.

Friedan, Betty. *The Feminine Mystique.* New York: W.W. Norton, 1963.

Frisken, Amanda. "Sexual Politics in Reconstruction: The Woodhull Years, 1970–1876," unpublished dissertation, State University of New York at Stony Brook, 1999.

Gallichan, Walter M. *The Great Unmarried.* London: T. Werner Laurie, Ltd, 1915.

Goffman, Erving. *Frame Analysis.* New York: Harper, 1974.

Goldin, Claudia. *Understanding the Gender Gap: An Economic History of American Women.* New York: Oxford University Press, 1990.

Gordon, Linda. *Woman's Body, Woman's Right: Birth Control in America.* New York: Penguin Books, 1977.

Graham, Patricia A. "Expansion and Exclusion: A History of Women in American Higher Education." *Signs: Journal of Women in Culture and Society* 3:4 (1978), pp. 759–773.

Griswold, Jerry. *Audacious Kids: Coming of Age in America's Classic Children's Books.* New York: Oxford University Press, 1992.

Harding, M. Esther. *The Way of All Women: A Psychological Interpretation.* New York: Longmans, 1934.

Hausman, Bernice. "Sex Before Gender: Charlotte Perkins Gilman and the Revolutionary Pardigm of Utopia." *Feminist Studies* 24:3 (1998), pp. 488–510.

Hoff, Joan. *Law, Gender & Injustice: A Legal History of U.S. Women.* New York: New York University Press, 1991.

Hutton, Laura. *The Single Woman and Her Emotional Problems.* London: Bailliere, Tindall and Cox, 1937.

Jacoby, Russell. *Social Amnesia: A Critique of Conformist Psychoanalysis from Adler to Laing.* Boston: Beacon, 1975.

Jeffreys, Sheila. *The Spinster and Her Enemies: Feminism and Sexuality, 1880–1930.* London: Pandora, 1985.

Kaplan, E. Anne. "The Case of the Missing Mother." In Patricia Ehrens, ed., *Issues in Feminist Film Criticism.* Bloomington: Indiana University Press, 1990, pp. 126–136.

Kessler-Harris, Alice. *Out to Work: A History of Wage Earning Women in the United States.* New York: Oxford University Press, 1982.

Kinsey, Alfred et al. *Sexual Behavior in the Human Female.* Philadelphia: Saunders, 1953.

Kopytoff, Igor. "Women's Roles and Existential Identities." In Peggy Sanday and Ruth Goodenough, eds, *Beyond the Second Sex.* College Park: University of Pennsylvania Press, 1990, pp. 75–98.

Kornbluh, Felicia A. "The New Literature on Gender and the Welfare State: The U.S. Case. *Feminist Studies* 22:1 (1996), pp. 171–197.

Ladies Home Journal. Philadelphia: Curtis Publishing Company, 1873– .

Laqueur, Thomas. *Making Sex: Body and Gender from the Greeks to Freud.* Cambridge: Harvard University Press, 1990.

Lancaster, Roger N., and Micaela di Leonardo. *The Gender/Sexuality Reader.* New York: Routledge, 1997.

Laurents, Arthur. *Time of the Cuckoo*. New York: Random House (originally produced 1951), 1953.

Leach, William. *True Love and Perfect Union: The Feminist Reform of Sex and Society*. Middletown: Weslyan University Press, 1989.

Lewis, Mayone. "A Defense of the Spinster." *Harpers Magazine* 137:1918, pp. 821–82.

Luce, Clair Booth. *The Women*. New York: Dramatists Play Service, 1937.

Lundberg, Ferdinand, and Marynia F. Farnham. *Modern Woman: The Lost Sex*, New York: Harper & Bros, 1947.

MacLeod, Arlene Elowe. "Accommodating Protest: Working Women, the New Veiling, and Change in Cairo." *Signs: Journal of Women in Culture and Society* 20:1 (1994), pp. 223–228.

Marks, Patricia. *Bicycles, Bangs, and Bloomers: The New Woman in the Popular Press*. Lexington: The University Press of Kentucky, 1990.

Markus, Hazel, and Paula Nurius, "Possible Selves," *American Psychologist*, September, 41:9 (1986), pp. 954–969.

Mason, Michael. *The Making of Victorian Sexuality*. Oxford: Oxford University Press, 1995.

Matthews, Glenna. *The Rise of Public Woman: Woman's Power and Woman's Place in the United States 1630–1970*. New York: Oxford University Press, 1992.

May, Elaine Tyler. *Barren in the Promised Land: Childless Americans and the Pursuit of Happiness*. Basic Books, 1995.

———. "Explosive Issues," in *Recasting America: Culture and Politics in the Age of the Cold War*. Lary May, ed. Chicago: University of Chicago Press, 1989, pp. 154–170.

May, Lary. *Screening Out the Past: The Birth of Mass Culture and the Motion Picture Industry*. Chicago: University of Chicago Press, 1983.

McCauley, Laurence James. *The Single Woman*. New York: Duell, Sloan & Pearce, 1952.

Mellencamp, Patricia. *A Fine Romance: Five Ages of Film Feminism*. Philadelphia: Temple University Press, 1995.

Modleski, Tania. "A Woman's Gotta Do . . . What a Man's Gotta Do? Cross-Dressing in the Western." *Signs: Journal of Women in Culture and Society* 22:3 (1997), pp. 519–544.

Morantz-Sanchez, Regina. *Sympathy and Science: Women Physicians in American Medicine*. Oxford: Oxford University Press, 1985.

O'Neill, William. *Everyone Was Brave: A History of Feminism in American*. Chicago: Quadrangle Books, 1969.

Onions, C. T. *Shorter Oxford English Dictionary on Historical Principles*. Oxford: Oxford University Press, 1939.

Oppenheimer, Valerie K. *The Female Labor Force in the United States*. Population Monograph Series, no. 5. Berkeley: University of California Press, 1970.

Oram, Alison. "Repressed and Thwarted, or Bearer of the New World? The Spinster in Inter-war Feminist Discourses." *Women's History Review* 1:3 (1992), pp. 413–434.

Peterson, Nancy. *Our Lives for Ourselves: Women Who Have Never Married*. New York: Putnam's Sons, 1981.

Pfister, Joel, and Nancy Schnog. *Inventing the Psychological: Toward a Cultural History of Emotional Life in America*. New Haven: Yale University Press, 1997.

Polletta, Francesca. " 'It Was Like a Fever . . .' Narrative and Identity in Social Protest." *Social Problems* 45:2 (1998), pp. 137–159.

Prouty, Olive. *Now, Voyager*. New York: Random House, 1941.

Reskin, Barbara F., and Polly Phillips. "Women in Male-Dominated Professions and Managerial Occupations." In Ann Stromberg and Shirley Harkness, eds. *Women Working,* 2nd ed. Mountain View, CA: Mayfield Press, 1989, pp. 190–205.

Rich, Adrienne. "Compulsory Heterosexuality and Lesbian Existence." *Signs: Journal of Women in Culture and Society* 5:4 (1981), pp. 713–736.

Rosen, Marjorie. *Popcorn Venus: Women, Movies and the American Dream.* New York: Coward, McCann and Geoghegan, 1973.

Rosenthal, Naomi, Meryl Fingrutd, Roberta Karant, Michele Ethier, and David McDonald. "Social Movements and Network Analysis: A Case Study of Nineteenth Century Women's Reform in New York State." *American Journal of Sociology* 90:5 (1985), pp. 1022–1054.

Rothman, Sheila M. *Woman's Proper Place: A History of Changing Ideals and Practices, 1870 to the Present.* New York: Basic Books, 1978.

Rupp, Leila J. "Sexuality and Politics in the Early Twentieth Century: The Case of the International Women's Movement." *Feminist Studies* 23:3 (1997), pp. 577–606.

Scanlon, Jennifer. *Inarticulate Longings: The Ladies' Home Journal, Gender, and the Promises of Consumer Culture.* New York: Routledge, 1995.

Searles, Patricia, and Janet Mickish. " 'A Thoroughbred Girl:' Images of Female Gender Role in Turn of the Century Mass Media." *Women's Studies* 3 (1984), pp. 261–81.

Seidman, Steven. *Romantic Longings: Love in America. 1830–1980.* New York: Routledge, 1991.

Shaw, Anna Howard, with Elizabeth Jordan. *Story of a Pioneer.* New York: Harper and Brothers, 1915.

Sicherman, Barbara. "College and Careers: Historical Perspectives on the Life and Work Patterns of Women College Graduates." In John Faragher and Florence Howe, eds., *Women and Higher Education in America.* New York: W.W. Norton, 1988.

Simmons, Christina. "Modern Sexuality and the Myth of Victorian Repression," in Kathy Peiss and Christina Simmons, eds., *Passion and Power: Sexuality in History.* Philadelpia: Temple University Press, 1989, pp. 157–177.

Simon, Barbara Levy. *Never Married Women.* Philadelphia: Temple University Press, 1987.

Solomon, Barbara M. *In the Company of Educated Women: A History of Women and Higher Education in America.* New Haven: Yale University Press, 1985.

Smith, Daniel Scott. "The Dating of the American Sexual Revolution: Evidence and Interpretation." In Michael Gordon, ed., *The American Family in Social-Historical Perspective,* 2nd ed. New York: St. Martin's Press, 1978, pp. 426–443.

———. "Family Limitation, Sexual Control, and Domestic Feminism in Victorian America." In Nancy F. Cott and Elizabeth Pleck, eds., *A Heritage of Her Own: Toward a New Social History of American Women.* New York: Simon and Shuster, 1979, pp. 222–245.

Smith, Dorothy. "Femininity as Discourse." In L. Roman and L. K. Christian-Smith, eds., *Becoming Feminine: The Politics of Popular Culture.* Philadelphia: Falmer, 1988.

Smith, M. B. *The Single Woman of Today: Her Problems and Adjustment.* London: Watts & Co, 1951.

Smith, Page. *Killing the Spirit: Higher Education in America.* New York: Penguin, 1990.

Smith-Rosenberg, Carrol. *Disorderly Conduct: Visions of Gender in Victorian America.* Oxford: Oxford University Press, 1985.

Stacey, Judith. "Virtual Truth with a Vengance." *Contemporary Sociology* 28:2 (1999), pp. 18–23.

Storey, John. *Cultural Studies and the Study of Popular Culture: Theories and Methods.* Athens: University of Georgia Press, 1996.

Stricker, Frank. "Cookbooks and Law Books: The Hidden History of Career Women in Twentieth Century America." *Journal of Social History* 10:1 (1976), pp. 1–19.

Susman, Warren. *Culture as History: The Transformation of American Society in the 20th Century.* New York: Pantheon, 1984.

Swidler, Ann. "Culture in Action: Symbols and Strategies." *American Journal of Sociology* 51:2 (1986), pp. 273–286.

Tebbel, John, and Mary Ellen Zuckerman. *The Magazine in America, 1741–1990.* New York: Oxford University Press, 1991.

Tilton, Robert S. *Pocahontas: The Evolution of an American Narrative.* New York: Cambridge University Press, 1994.

Todd, Janet. *Women and Film.* New York: Holmes and Meier, 1988.

Tractenberg, Alan. *The Incorporation of America: Culture and Society in the Gilded Age.* New York: Hill and Wang, 1982.

Turner, Graeme. *Film as Social Practice.* London: Routledge, 1993.

Turner, Victor. *Dramas, Fields, Metaphors: Symbolic Action in Human Society,* Ithaca: Cornell University Press, 1974.

Ullman, Sharon R. *Sex Seen: The Emergence of Modern Sexuality in America.* Berkeley: University of California Press, 1997.

U.S. Bureau of the Census. *Historical Statistics of the United States, Colonial Times to 1970.* Washington, DC: U.S. Department of Commerce, 1976.

———. *Statistical Abstract of the United States,* Washington, DC: U.S. Department of Commerce, 1992.

Van de Velde, Theodore. *Ideal Marriage: Its Physiology and Techniques.* Stella Braun, translator. New York: Random House, 1930.

Walsh, Mary. *Doctors Wanted, No Women Need Apply: Barriers in the Medical Profession, 1835–1975.* New Haven: Yale University Press, 1977.

Watkins, Susan Cotts. "Spinsters." *Journal of Family History 9:2* (1984), pp. 310–324.

Wharton, Edith. *The Old Maid (Old New York: The 'Fifties).* New York: D. Appleton and Co. (reprinted from *Redbook Magazine,* 1922), 1924.

Who's Who in America. Chicago: Marquis Publishing, 1914 and 1933.

Wolman, Benjamin B., ed. *Encyclopedia of Psychiatry, Psychology and Psychoanalysis.* New York: Holt, 1996.

Wylie, Phillip. *Generation of Vipers,* New York: Rinehart, 1942.

Zylan, Yvonne. "Comment on Fraser and Gordon's 'A Geneology of Dependency: Tracing a Keyword of the U.S. Welfare State." *Signs: Journal of Women in Culture and Society* 21:2, (1996), pp. 515–530.

FILMOGRAPHY

Father Was a Fullback. Directed by John M. Stahl, with Fred MacMurray and Maureen O'Hara, 1949.

It's a Wonderful Life. Directed by Frank Capra, with James Stewart and Donna Reed, 1946.

Now, Voyager. Directed by Irving Rapper, with Bette Davis and Paul Heinreid, 1942.

Plaza Suite. Directed by Arthur Heller, with Walter Matthau and Maureen Stapleton. 1969.

Rebel Without a Cause. Directed by Nicholas Ray, with James Dean, Natalie Wood, and Sal Mineo. 1955.

Summertime. Directed by David Lean, with Katherine Hepburn and Rossano Brazzi, 1955.

Suspicion. Directed by Alfred Hitchcock, with Cary Grant and Joan Fontaine, 1941.

The Women. Directed by George Cukor, with Norma Shearer, Joan Crawford, and Rosalind Russell, 1939.

INDEX